WORLD BANK WORKING PAPER

Regulation by Contract

A New Way to Privatize Electricity Distribution?

Tonci Bakovic
Bernard Tenenbaum
Fiona Woolf

THE WORLD BANK
Washington, D.C.

printed on
recycled
paper

1 2 3 4 05 04 03

ISBN: 0-8213-5592-9
eISBN: 0-8213-5593-7
ISSN: 1726-5878

Tonci Bakovic is Senior Energy Specialist in the Investment Division at the International Financial Corporation. Bernard Tenenbaum is Lead Energy Specialist in the Energy and Water Department at the World Bank. Fiona Wolf is Senior Partner for Energy Practice at CMS Cameron McKenna.

Library of Congress Cataloging-in-Publication Data

Bakovic, Tonci, 1963-
    Regulation by contract: a new way to privatize electricity distribution? / Tonci Bakovic, Bernard Tenenbaum, Fiona Wolf.
        p. cm.-- (World Bank working paper; 14)
    Includes bibliographical references.
    ISBN 0-8213-5592-9
    1. Electric utilities--Law and legislation. 2. Privatization--Law and legislation. 3. Concessions. 4. Independent regulatory commissions. 5. Electric power distribution. I. Tenenbaum, Bernard William. II. Woolf, Fiona, 1948- III. Title. IV. World Bank working Paper; no. 14.

K3982.B35 2003
343.09'29--dc21   2003057150

TABLE OF CONTENTS

BOXES

TABLES

FOREWORD

The worldwide movement towards power sector reform in developing countries began more than ten years ago. Usually, the reforms have involved some combination of restructuring, privatization and unbundling. Regulatory reform has also been a key element of the overall reform package. In almost every instance, the principal recommendation for regulatory reform has been to create an "independent regulatory agency."

The motivation for this recommendation was straightforward. It was thought that successful power sector reform required depoliticizing the tariff-setting process and that an independent regulatory commission would be best able to do this. While there is still general acceptance that implementation of tariff-setting in the power sector must be depoliticized (that is, made more of a technical than a political exercise) if the overall reform is to be sustainable, there is also a growing consensus, achieved with the benefit of the hindsight, that "independence is not enough" to achieve this goal.

In particular, there is growing realization that regulatory independence, while still very important, must be combined with a clearly specified tariff framework. Or, to put it in another way, independence does *not* mean that a newly created regulatory commission should have total discretion in deciding on the substance and process of post-reform tariff setting. The key lesson of the last years is that independence, by itself, does not create regulatory commitment. Therefore, the principal recommendation of this paper is that *regulatory independence should be combined with a clearly specified regulatory contract that must be negotiated by political authorities*. This is, in effect, a recommendation that successful power sector reform in World Bank client countries requires the combination of two distinct regulatory traditions—the Anglo-American tradition of independent regulatory entities with the French tradition of a well-specified regulatory contract or concession agreement.

The specific focus of the paper is on how regulatory contracts can be combined with independent regulatory commissions to promote successful privatization of electricity distribution. The essence of the regulatory contract is a pre-specification in one or more formal or explicit agreements of the formulas and procdures that determine the prices that a distribution company will be allowed to charge for the electricity that it sells. Regulatory contracts are not a new concept. Regulatory contracts have been combined with independent or partially independent regulatory commissions in many Latin American countries, and this combination has generally been successful in inducing and sustaining private sector investment in more than 60 privatizations of electricity distribution systems.

The paper goes beyond general principles. It provides a wealth of details on how specific features of regulatory contracts have been implemented in various countries and the lessons that can be drawn from this experience. In particular, it reviews the experience of several countries, with special emphasis on how certain key design elements (for example, pass-through of power purchase costs, foreign exchange fluctuations, technical and commercial loss reductions and obligation to serve) are dealt with in regulatory contracts. It examines why the regulatory contracts in Brazil have been less successful than those in other Latin American countries. Because disagreements are almost inevitable in any contract, the paper also considers the strengths and weaknesses of several traditional and non-traditional approaches to dealing with disputes. While the paper's focus is on the design and implementation of regulatory contracts, it points out that regulatory contracts, by themselves, are not a "magic solution." No regulatory contract, no matter how well designed, will be sustainable unless there is a reasonable likelihood that the regulated enterprise's revenues will cover its costs.

I believe that this paper makes a major contribution to our understanding of issues in developing countries because it provides important and practical insights on how regulation can and should be practiced. Most people would agree that the sustainability of any regulatory system ultimately depends on its success in providing investors with "confidence" and consumers with "protection." This paper provides a number of ideas on how both of these goals can be achieved. I would like to commend the three authors for bringing focus and clarity to an important debate that will be of interest to anyone who is concerned with the future of power sector reform in developing countries.

Jamal Saghir
Director, Energy and Water
Chairman, Energy and Mining Sector Board

ABSTRACT

In many developing countries, both governments and investors have expressed disappointment with the performance of recently privatized electricity distribution companies. Governments complain that tariffs have increased without visible improvements in service. Investors contend that they have not earned reasonable returns on their investments. Both sides often express dissatisfaction with the new independent regulatory commissions established at the time of privatization. In particular, investors argue that the commissions have not lived up to their commitments and almost always side with consumer interests.

Some investors claim that the design of the new regulatory system in many developing and transition economies is fundamentally flawed. They often recommend that independent regulatory commissions be supplemented or replaced by more explicit "regulation by contract."

This paper examines whether regulation by contract or a combination of regulation by contract and regulatory independence would provide a better regulatory system for developing countries that wish to privatize some or all of their distribution systems. The paper:

- Describes the key characteristics of regulation by contract as it has been implemented in several developing countries
- Focuses on how regulatory contracts in several countries handle certain key issues (pass-through of power-purchase costs, foreign exchange fluctuations, loss reduction and the obligation to serve)
- Describes the strengths and weaknesses of different approaches for dealing with disputes that inevitably arise in the application of regulatory contracts
- Compares and contrasts some recent experiences of distribution entities in Latin America and India. Examines some of Brazil's recent problems that may have arisen because Brazil adopted a flawed variant of regulation by contract.

The paper concludes with a discussion of some lessons that can be learned from the experience of several countries.

ACKNOWLEDGMENTS

This paper could not have been written without the assistance of many friends and colleagues inside and outside the World Bank. These individuals helped to develop an understanding of power sector and regulatory reforms in developing and developed countries. They gave freely of their time and insights to make sure that we got the facts right and understood what the facts really meant. They include: Manish Agarwal, Beatriz Arizu, Ian Alexander, Pedro Antmann, José-Maria Bakovic, John Besant-Jones, Laurent Durix, Phillip Gray, Mohinder Gulati, Amit Kapur, Chris Shugart, Alan Townsend, Luiz Maurer and Joseph Wright. Of course, none of them should be held responsible for any errors of fact or interpretation that remain despite their best efforts to educate us.

Anne Vroom provided cheerful and timely assistance in the production of the paper while also providing mini-tutorials on the intricacies of MS Word. Chris Marquardt was an excellent editor who constantly reminded us that our goal was to communicate information and ideas to a wide audience and not just to write another report.

Finally, we wish to acknowledge the financial assistance of the World Bank's Energy and Water Department in preparing this report. We owe a special debt of gratitude to the department's director, Jamal Saghir. It was Jamal's suggestion that we look at this topic. We naively said that we would get back to him in a week or two with a short note. When it became clear that the topic merited more than a few pages, Jamal encouraged us to wrestle with the issues and seek out real world examples even if it meant that the one-week project eventually became a multi-month effort.

Authors

Tonci Bakovic (tbakovic@ifc.org) is a Senior Energy Specialist in the Investments Division at the International Finance Corporation. Before joining the IFC, he was the Power Sector Reform Coordinator for the World Bank in Bolivia and then Dominion Energy's Business Development Manager for Latin America. Mr. Bakovic co-wrote the Bolivian Electricity Law on a leave of absence from Ernst & Young.

Bernard Tenenbaum (btenenbaum@worldbank.org) is a Lead Energy Specialist in the Energy and Water Department at the World Bank. Before joining the World Bank, he served as the Deputy Associate Director of the Office of Economic Policy at the U.S. Federal Energy Regulatory Commission.

Fiona Woolf (fiona.woolf@cmck.com) is a senior partner in the Energy Practice at CMS Cameron McKenna. She has acted as a legal and policy advisor on issues relating to power sector reform and regulation in more than 30 separate countries or jurisdictions. She recently authored a book titled *Global Transmission Expansion: Recipes for Success* (PennWell) that compares transmission pricing and expansion policies across several countries.

Acronyms and Abbreviations

ADR	Alternative Dispute Resolution
disco	distribution company
FERC	Federal Energy Regulatory Commission
genco	generation company
ICC	International Chamber of Commerce
LCIA	London Court of International Arbitration
MIGA	Multilateral Investment Guarantee Agency
O&M	operations and maintenance
PPA	power purchase agreement
PRG	partial risk guarantee
SOE	state-owned [power] enterprise
transco	transmission company
UNCITRAL	U.N. Commission on International Trade Law

EXECUTIVE SUMMARY

The last few years have not been kind to investors in recently privatized electricity distribution companies in developing countries. Governments and consumers have expressed disappointment with the companies' performance, as well as with the new independent regulatory commissions established to regulate the companies. Investors have also been disappointed. They argue that the commissions have not lived up to their commitments and almost always side with consumer interests.

Following several widely publicized setbacks, many investors are questioning whether private investment in electricity distribution is viable in most developing countries. Meanwhile, many consumers are now actively opposed to distribution privatization. In fact, the opposition is so strong that some governments are fearful of even using the word *privatization*.

In light of these events, it is reasonable to ask: What has gone wrong?

The key lesson of the last years is that regulatory independence, by itself, creates neither regulatory commitment nor balanced decisionmaking. The principal lesson learned is that independence is not enough. Regulatory independence must be combined with a *clearly specified regulatory contract that must be negotiated by political authorities*. In effect, the authors recommend combining two distinct regulatory traditions—the Anglo-American tradition of independent regulatory entities and the French tradition of a well-specified regulatory contract or concession agreement.

This paper goes beyond general principles. It provides a wealth of details on how specific features of regulatory contracts have been implemented in various developing countries and the lessons that can be drawn from this experience. Particular emphasis is placed on how certain key design elements—pass-through of power purchase costs, foreign exchange fluctuations, technical and commercial loss reductions and obligation to serve—are dealt with in regulatory contracts.

Regulatory Independence

The World Bank has been encouraging its client countries to create independent regulatory commissions since the issuance of its power sector policy paper in 1993. However, the expected benefit of independent regulatory commissions following general tariff principles—a commercially viable power sector that benefits both consumers and investors—has not been realized. The reality is that raising tariffs for retail customers is a politically charged exercise in the Bank's client countries—usually low-income countries whose existing electricity tariffs often fall far short of covering costs. It has been almost impossible for new regulatory systems to operate as planned in the first years of their existence.

Regulation by Contract

Some observers have recommended *regulation by contract* as an alternative to regulatory independence. The essence of regulation by contract is pre-specification, in one or more formal or explicit agreements, of the formulas that determine prices that a distribution company is allowed to charge for the electricity it sells. This does *not* mean that the actual prices are pre-specified. What is pre-specified is the regulatory *treatment* (such as indexing, automatic pass-through or case-by-case determination) for the individual cost elements that together determine the retail tariff.

The application of this general concept has yielded different operational definitions. One definition is "regulation without a regulator." A second definition, and one that is used in this paper, is "a detailed tariff-setting agreement administered by an independent regulator." Under this definition, *the regulatory contract does not replace the regulator but substantially limits the regulator's discretion*. In particular, it forces the regulator to set tariffs based on specific formulas rather than just general principles.

Some private investors have argued that there already exists a working model in the power sector for regulation by contract: the numerous *power purchase agreements* (*PPAs*) that currently exist. In fact, regulatory contracts in distribution are more difficult to negotiate and sustain than PPAs because of the large number of customers, the high visibility of the retail price and the need for ongoing investments. Nonetheless, the success of some Latin American countries suggests that regulatory contracts for electricity distribution can and should be negotiated.

To be sustainable, regulation by contract must achieve two goals: it must (1) protect consumers from monopoly prices and inferior quality of service while also (2) attracting investors who will make the investments to provide the service at affordable prices. The objective is to have the best of both worlds and to define the trade-offs between these two conflicting regulatory objectives. The idea is to limit the discretion of the regulator in areas that are known to deter investment while at the same time using independent regulation to avoid uncertainties for investors created by political micro-management and changes of government or governmental policy.

The key component of the regulatory contract is a performance-based, multi-year tariff-setting system. *The concept of independence does not logically require that a regulatory commission design the tariff system that it implements.* In many Latin American countries, independent or quasi-independent regulatory commissions have been administering tariff-setting systems that were established by governments before the commissions came into existence.

Real-World Regulatory Experiences: Brazil and India

The most prominent example of regulation by contract in developing countries can be found in the more than 60 distribution privatizations that have occurred throughout Latin America over the last 15 years. But whereas Latin American countries have generally had success with regulation by contract, Brazil has encountered major regulatory and economic problems with its particular approach. The Brazilian experience provides some lessons on "what not to do" with regulatory contracts:

1. Vagueness in tariff-setting provisions
2. Uncertainty about pass-through for power-purchase costs
3. Low allowed prices for pass-through of power-purchase costs
4. Foreign exchange risk
5. Uncertainty in the legal framework
6. Lack of respect for contracts

The Indian regulatory system has suffered from different flaws. It is based on an annual cost-of-service approach that gives considerable discretion to the regulators. It has been recommended that Indian regulators move to a form of "regulation by contract" for potential private distribution companies that would be more akin to what exists in Latin America and elsewhere. As in Latin America, the key elements of the proposed system would be (1) automatic pass-through of cost elements that are largely beyond the distribution entity's control (such as power purchases and taxes) and (2) indexing and efficiency targets for cost elements that can be controlled (such as losses and labor costs).

Unfortunately, under most current Indian proposals, multi-year tariffs would be *permitted* rather than *required*. However, this would still leave considerable uncertainty compared to other countries. The better solution for India would probably be to amend the existing state electricity reform acts to mandate the use of multi-year tariffs—or, even better, to (1) transfer tariff-setting authority back to the government on a one-time basis for the initial post-privatization period, (2) incorporate the tariff-setting formula directly into the privatization agreement (which is the norm in almost every other country that has successfully privatized distribution) and (3) establish, via amendments to the existing state electricity laws, fairly detailed tariff principles and processes that would apply to subsequent multi-year tariff periods. Without such changes, any privatization will take place under a cloud of legal uncertainty.

The Details of the Regulatory Contract, or Who Bears What Risk?

Many of the disagreements in designing a regulatory contract involve disagreements over whether the company, its customers or the government should bear a particular risk. From a potential investor's perspective, the allocation of risk in the regulatory contract will ultimately affect one of three things: the prices that it can charge, the costs that it can recover, and the quantity of electricity that it can sell.

It is generally agreed that the best principle for risk allocation is that a particular risk should be borne by the party that can mitigate or manage the risk at the lowest cost. Although the principle is easy to state, there is often considerable disagreement over how it should be applied in particular situations. This can be seen in a detailed analysis of four such key risks:

- *Pass-through of power-purchase costs.* Partial or delayed pass-through of power-purchase costs could bankrupt a distribution company because these costs usually constitute about 50 to 80 percent of its total costs. For this reason most private investors seek total and automatic pass-through of all power-purchase costs, arguing that such costs are largely beyond their control. In contrast, regulators generally fear that automatic pass-through will lead to corruption and inefficiency and, therefore, want the company to bear some risk of non-recovery through a benchmark or some other regulatory mechanism. Any regulatory mechanism designed to encourage economical purchasing—such as a cap on the prices paid for power purchases—will inevitably affect the incentives to build new generating capacity. Generally, a multi-market benchmark (Columbia and the Netherlands) seems preferable to a single, spot-market benchmark.
- *Loss-reduction targets.* The quantity of power purchases that the regulator will allow the disco to recover in tariffs depends largely on the *level of technical and commercial losses* on the disco system that is deemed to be acceptable. In India, recent estimates of overall

losses for some of the existing state-owned distribution systems are as high as 50 percent. In dealing with losses, the two key design questions in a regulatory contract are: 1) What should be the initial accepted level of overall losses for tariff-setting purposes? 2) How quickly can losses be reduced? The answers to these two questions determine how the cost of losses is allocated between the company and its customers. Privatized distribution companies in several Latin American countries have been very successful in reducing losses. This has largely been due to a high degree of control over the labor force and support from government and local police—conditions that might not exist to the same extent in India, Africa or elsewhere.

■ *Foreign exchange fluctuations.* Distribution companies receive payments from their customers in local currency but often incur costs in hard currencies. This leads to two major risks for private investors. The first risk—*convertibility* risk—is that the government will not give the distribution company access to sufficient foreign exchange to pay for costs incurred in hard currencies. The second risk—*exchange rate* risk—is that the local currency will lose value relative to hard currencies. Local-currency revenues may no longer be sufficient to cover foreign currency costs. *Indexing* is the most common and transparent way to deal with exchange-rate risk. If the local currency loses value relative to the hard currency, the government allows the disco to increase its tariffs by the amount necessary to cover the costs incurred in hard currencies. In theory, this transfers the risk to the distribution company's consumers. Whether this happens in practice depends critically on the extent of indexing and the frequency of adjustments.

■ *Obligation to supply. Obligation to serve* goes by different names, including *supply obligation* and *public service obligation.* The definition of obligation to serve cannot and should not be the same across all countries, and a system's *starting conditions* must be considered in defining an appropriate obligation (these include geographic scope, quality of service, and whether the obligation is absolute or limited). The obligation to serve has often failed in state-owned systems because of lack of money, ongoing political interference in operating and investment decisions, and, perhaps most important, lack of performance-based salary incentives. In designing the regulatory contract for the new private owner, *key questions* to ask include: Who must be served? What are the initial and phased in technical and commercial standards for service? What are the penalties if the company fails to meet these standards? Are excuses allowed?

Dealing with Disputes

A distribution utility can be involved in many disputes. The three principal types of disputes are those between the distribution company and its customers, between the distribution company and other industry participants, and between the distribution company and its regulator. This paper focuses on the last type—disputes between the distribution and the regulator over either the substance of the regulator's decisions or the process by which the regulator reached these decisions. The various approaches to resolving disputes include the following:

■ *The local court system.* Local courts are generally not viable for dealing with regulatory disputes because they are slow, lack the requisite knowledge, and are sometimes corrupt.

■ *International arbitration.* This is a necessary and appropriate backstop for regulatory disputes in countries with no track record for impartial resolution of such disputes. However, it is best held in reserve as a last resort for dealing with disputes. Its principal value is derived from the simple fact that it exists, even if it is never used.

■ *Mediation.* Alternative Dispute Resolution (ADR), of which mediation is the most common form, typically involves the facilitation of structured efforts (such as expert panels and mediation) by the parties to settle dispute for themselves without going to a local court. However, no binding resolution can occur unless and until an agreement is reached and committed to writing. In general, it does not work for regulatory disputes because regulators have little or no incentive to enter into mediation.

▪ *Expert panels.* To adopt expert panels for regulatory contracts, the distributor must have the unilateral right to convene the panel, and there must be an effective mechanism for enforcing the experts' decision. One promising hybrid technique is to create a standing expert panel that can act as both an expert fact-finding panel and arbitration panel.

▪ *A specialized appeals tribunal.* To date, the real-world experience with special appellate tribunals in most countries has generally been positive. They tend to produce quick, well-informed, inexpensive decisions, and can be created without having to reform the existing court system.

To enforce decisions, an existing World Bank financing instrument known as a *partial risk guarantee* (PRG) may prove useful. Other guarantee instruments have been offered by the World Bank's Multilateral Investment Guarantee Agency (MIGA) to provide insurance against currency inconvertibility, breach or repudiation of contract and expropriation. It has been recommended that a new type of guarantee be created to backstop the operation of regulatory systems. Specifically, the proposed PRG would guarantee scheduled payments of principal and interest payments on debt if the private investor defaults on or delays payments because the regulator fails to honor the terms of the regulatory contract. However, the viability of such a PRG will depend critically on the clarity and comprehensiveness of the regulatory contract.

Concluding Observations

Ten key lessons have been learned from the experience of developing and developed countries with regulation by contract:

1. *Independence is not enough.* Ten years of experience indicate that true regulatory independence often falls victim to direct or indirect political pressures to avoid actions that a government thinks will be politically damaging. Even where regulatory independence has been achieved, the regulators in developing countries will find it difficult to make balanced decisions because starting conditions are bad, transitions take longer than expected, the government does not pay its bills or enforce law and order, and foreign ownership is viewed as a new form of colonialism. The single most important lesson is that independence must be "backstopped" by a regulatory contract that goes beyond general principles. The key element of the regulatory contract should be a well-specified, multi-year tariff-setting system that is required by law and specified in concessions, licenses and other regulatory instruments.

2. *The regulatory contract must be a political contract.* Commitment will not be believable unless it comes from the country's highest political authorities. However, once the regulatory contract is in place (in effect, the political deal has been made), the contract is best administered by an independent regulator. The underlying principles and initial parameters of the regulatory contract should be clearly specified in the country's primary or secondary electricity laws (Argentina, Bolivia, Chile, Peru). A regulatory contract is less likely to survive if it is poorly specified (Brazil) or exists only within a stand-alone concession or license agreement (Brazil).

3. *"Regulation by contract versus regulation by commission" is a false dichotomy.* The real choice is between an independent regulator with substantial discretion and an independent regulator with little discretion, especially in the first post-privatization tariff period. An independent regulator should set prices under a well-specified, pre-determined, multi-year tariff-setting system, and recommendations should be transparent.

4. *Regulation by contract is a new name for an old paradigm.* Regulation by contract—an independent or quasi-independent regulator administering a well-specified tariff-setting

system that is embedded in laws, concessions and regulations—has been the norm for distribution privatizations throughout Latin America for more than 15 years.

5. *Electricity consumers cannot be the forgotten third party to a regulatory contract.* The government and regulator must ensure a fair balance between the interests of consumers and those of investors. If consumers fail to see any obvious benefits from the regulatory contract ("early wins"), it will be politically unsustainable.

6. *Investors must have confidence that the contract will be enforced fairly and efficiently.* It is preferable to combine the "backstop" of international arbitration with less costly forms of dispute resolution that can prevent one or more smaller disputes from exploding into a big dispute.

7. *The heart of a regulatory contract is a pre-specified, performance based, multi-year tariff-setting system.* This should include benchmarks or targets for controllable costs and automatic pass-through for non-controllable costs.

8. *A regulatory contract is sustainable only if the underlying economics are viable.* Regulation by contract will not work if there is a large gap between costs and revenues. The gap must be closed by lowering costs, increasing revenues, or both. Investors must be protected, and the regulatory contract might need to be combined with transition-period subsidies (with help from World Bank loans or guarantees).

9. *A multi-year tariff system can be put into operation even in the absence of high-quality data.* Data quality will improve through privatization, especially if "better data" is specified as a performance element in the regulatory contract. If there is a political concern that investors will be able to earn high profits because of poor data quality, then the tariff system should include a within–tariff-period "sharing" mechanism between the distribution companies and its customers.

10. *Regulation by contract should be reserved for private distribution companies.* In most developing countries, state-owned enterprises do not respond to normal commercial incentives. Thus there is little to be gained in creating a new independent regulator to regulate a state-owned power enterprise.

Appendixes
Appendixes A, B and C contain text for a proposed statute in a South Asian country that contains some elements—governing controllable and non-controllable costs, obligation to serve, and quality of service—of the legal foundation of a regulatory contract.

CHAPTER 1

INTRODUCTION

"Governments throughout the world engage in three main activities: they tax, they spend and they regulate. Regulation is the least understood...."[1]

Recent Events

The last few years have not favored private investors in electricity distribution companies in developing countries. In India, the AES Corporation told the Orissa state government that it wished to sell its ownership interest in a local distribution company because it saw no way to make the company a viable commercial enterprise. A few months later, BSES, a large Indian power company that had invested in three other distribution companies in Orissa, also threatened to leave. In Ecuador, the government announced that it was abandoning its plans to privatize 17 state electricity distribution companies after receiving a poll that showed that more than 71 percent of the general public was opposed to such privatizations. In Senegal, a new government terminated its agreement with Senelec, a consortium of Tractebel/Hydro Quebec, after accusing the consortium of failing to improve the frequency and duration of blackouts. In Brazil, AES experienced major financial problems for Electropaulo, its distribution company in Sao Paulo—problems caused in part by a significant drop in sales and revenues following in the wake of a government-mandated rationing program. The company protested that the rationing program put it in the difficult position of having to tell its customers: "We are asking you not to buy the only thing that we have to sell."[2]

---

1. Scott Jacobs, *Building Regulatory Institutions: The Search for Legitimacy and Efficiency* (OECD, Center for Cooperation with Economies in Transition, Paris, 1994).

2. "Power Policemen: Electricity Rationing Roils Brazil, Leaving U.S. Utility in a Spot," *Wall Street Journal,* July 30, 2001, p. 1. Other private distribution companies have also had problems in Brazil. In August 2002, CEMAR, a subsidiary of the U.S. company PPL, declared bankruptcy. In addition, there have been reports of several multinational energy companies wanting to leave. See "8 Utilities In Brazil Could Go On The Block," *New York Times,* August 30, 2002, Section V, p. 1.

With these widely publicized setbacks, many investors are now questioning whether private investment in electricity distribution is viable in most developing countries. And many consumers are actively opposed to distribution privatization. In fact, the opposition is so strong that some governments are fearful of even using the word *privatization*.[3] In light of these events, it is reasonable to ask: What has gone wrong?

The Wrong Advice?

Investors frequently maintain that these failures stem from flaws in many of the more than 50 new electricity regulatory systems recently established in developing countries.[4] There has been too much emphasis, they argue, on creating "independent regulatory commissions" as the key to successful distribution privatization. They contend that this is a naïve recommendation for most developing countries. At a recent privatization conference in India, for example, one Indian investor observed with exasperation that "regulatory independence is a fine concept, but it is of little comfort when I don't have enough money to pay my employees and creditors. I need money, not mantras."[5] Other investors have argued that the danger of an independent regulatory commission is that it can easily turn into a "rogue regulatory commission" especially if the commission operates under a law that specifies only general tariff-setting principles. They also contend that a new independent regulatory commission guided only by general tariff-setting principles will almost always favor the interests of consumers over those of investors because it will have too much discretion. In their view, the better alternative is "regulation through contract" rather than "independent regulatory commissions."[6]

Regulation by contract is an appealing concept because it seems to hold the promise of a regulatory system that operates on "autopilot." Private power investors like the idea because it looks familiar. It bears a strong resemblance to PPAs (power purchase agreements)—direct contracts between government enterprises and private generators for long-term bulk power sales—that are usually directly negotiated and implemented between the private investors and government. A typical PPA contains detailed formulas that specify the prices generators will be allowed to charge over the life of the contract. Regulators usually have little or nothing to do with either the design or the implementation of the PPAs. Not surprisingly, some private investors argue that if PPAs have been so successful in promoting private investment in generation, why can't the same regulatory technique be applied to distribution?

There is always a danger in replacing one mantra (independence) with another (regulation by contract). In this paper, we take a close look at whether "regulation by contract" is a viable regulatory approach for developing countries, either by itself or in combination with regulatory independence; and, if so, how it could be used to create new private distribution entities. The paper is organized as follows:

- ▪ Chapter 2 examines why regulatory independence was recommended by the World Bank and others. It also explores why regulatory independence, when combined with nothing more than general tariff principles, seems to have failed in developing countries.

---

3. Governments have become adept at creating euphemisms for privatization such as "disinvestment" (India), "ownership reform" (China), "peopleization" (Sri Lanka) and "equitization" (Vietnam), and "disincorporatization" (Mexico). See Nellis (2002).

4. In a recent survey of private investors, about 50 percent of the respondents said that their worst power sector investment experience was the failure of regulators to respect regulatory commitments. See Lamech and Saeed (2003).

5. Here and in several other places in this paper, we quote from individuals who provided comments "off the record."

6. Similar views can be found in the academic literature. See Levy and Spiller (1994), whose principal point is that a regulatory system must be compatible with a country's executive, legislative and institutional endowments. In practice, this means that many developing countries will need, at least initially, a well-specified and relatively inflexible regulatory contract.

- Chapter 3 describes the key characteristics of regulation by contract for electricity distribution companies as it has developed in several countries. It also discusses how regulation by contract differs from normal commercial contracts and considers whether the use of regulation by contract should be limited to just an initial, post-privatization transition period.
- Chapter 4 compares the recent real-world regulatory experiences of selected distribution entities in Latin America and India. It also takes a close look at recent problems in Brazil that may stem from a flawed variant of regulation by contract.
- Chapter 5 examines the details of actual regulatory contracts in several countries, especially with respect to the sharing of key risks such as pass-through of power-purchase costs, foreign exchange fluctuations, loss reduction and obligation to serve.
- Chapter 6 discusses alternative approaches to dealing with disputes that arise in the application of regulatory contracts.
- Chapter 7 suggests lessons learned.

Although the focus of this paper is on "good" and "bad" features of real-world regulatory systems, we do not believe that flawed regulation is the principal explanation for the disappointing performance of private companies in electricity distribution. Companies often use regulation as a convenient scapegoat to deflect attention away from their own strategic mistakes. For example, in Brazil and certain other countries it is now reasonably clear that some private companies paid too much for their investments and allowed themselves to become too highly leveraged. Although regulatory systems can and should be improved, such improvements will not save investors from their own mistakes.

CHAPTER 2

REGULATORY INDEPENDENCE

Why Encourage Regulatory Independence?

The World Bank has been encouraging its client countries to create independent regulatory commissions since the issuance of its power sector policy paper in 1993.[7] The reason for this was fairly straightforward: it was largely a reaction to the failures of a system of non-independent regulation that was the historic norm for most state-owned power enterprises (SOEs). Under this system, one or more government ministers would set both the level and structure of tariffs for SOEs. The final decision—usually made with the formal or informal approval of the country's president or prime minister—was often not published and rarely explained. Not surprisingly, this ministerial model of regulation usually produced tariffs that failed to cover costs because there were few, if any, political benefits to be gained by raising electricity prices.

When the Bank began to encourage privatization in the early 1990s, there was a consensus that private investors would not show up unless the system for setting tariffs—the core regulatory task—was "de-politicized" and "made independent." (These were euphemisms for a tariff-setting system that would balance consumer *and* investor interests.) Therefore, the Bank encouraged policy makers to create regulatory entities whose decisions would be both transparent and independent of government political authorities. The former meant that the new regulatory commission would publicly explain the reasons for its decisions and the latter meant that the commission would make tariff decisions under specified legal standards without getting the prior approval of a minister or prime minister.[8] It was hoped that this new tariff-setting system would produce better results because its decisions would be more technical than political. Yet, it was also recognized

---

7. World Bank (1993).

8. Although the Bank has tended to emphasize decision-making independence from government, full independence would also include independence from the regulated companies that are regulated and the customers that they serve. See Smith (1997).

that the new system would not work unless political authorities were willing to give up their existing control over electricity tariffs (that is, give up political power to get electrical power).

To be fair, the Bank's recommendation of regulatory independence was not categorical. A close reading of the 1993 power-sector policy statement shows that the Bank recommended "independence" only if the enterprise was first *corporatized* (allowed to make operating and investment decisions independent of political authorities) and *commercialized* (allowed to charge tariffs that recovered operating and capital costs). Although very few state power enterprises were ever successfully corporatized and commercialized, it appears that the regulatory recommendation was widely adopted. Fortunately, in actual operational work, Bank task managers rarely proposed independent regulatory commissions as a "stand-alone" option. More frequently, they recommended an independent regulatory commission combined with a pre-specified tariff-setting formula (a type of regulation by contract).[9]

What Went Wrong?

With the benefit of close to ten years of experience, we find that *the expected benefit of independent regulatory commissions following general tariff principles—a commercially viable power sector that benefits both consumers and investors—has not been realized.* The basic problem seems to be a "weak governance environment" (Levy and Spiller, 1994). This, in turn, has meant that new commissions have often failed to achieve independent and technical decision-making. Although new regulatory institutions have been created, it appears that in some countries "institutional change…changed nothing" or at least very little (Putnam, 1993). There seem to be at least three reasons for this failure:

1. *Many commissions never really became independent.* They may have looked independent on paper (i.e., had legally independent decision-making authority), but in reality many commissions have continued to operate as if they were still branches of one or more ministries. The behavior of the commissioners may have been influenced by the hope of a future higher-level job elsewhere in government (with the consequent need not to antagonize a minister when he called to discuss a pending tariff request), fear of losing their present jobs, continued government control over their budget, or a continuing antagonism to private ownership in a sector that had previously been largely public. Although one could say that the new commissions were "captured" by their governments, it is probably more accurate to say that the commissioners never really tried to become independent.

2. *Some commissions were granted only limited legal "independence."* In Hungary, Latvia and Lithuania, for example, the tariff-setting authority of the regulatory entity is formally limited to giving advice to a minister. In such a situation the regulator has, in effect, the legal right to give his opinion about tariffs but not much else. Elsewhere, regulators thought that they had independent and exclusive decision-making authority over tariff setting, but then discovered that the legislature, cabinet or president disagreed or did not care what the law said. In Georgia, after the regulatory commission issued a controversial tariff order, it was informed that the Parliament believed it could stop the order from going into effect.[10] In Pakistan, the cabinet of a new civilian government recently ordered a 5 percent tariff cut even though the authority to set tariffs had been transferred by law to NEPRA, the national electricity regulator.[11] In Bolivia, the president issued a decree

---

9. This has been the Bank's recommended approach in Bolivia, Georgia, Moldova, Peru, Uganda and, more recently, India.

10. Reuters Business Briefings, "Parliamentary Commission Criticizing Decision to Increase Electricity Tariff in Tbilisi," November 15, 2001.

11. Reuters News, "Pakistan Cuts Electricity Rates, Ignores Regulator, Sends Bad Signal To Investors," December 11, 2002.

freezing electricity tariffs after the regulator issued a notice that would have raised tariffs.[12] In all of these situations, the commission may have been legally independent but discovered that it was functionally irrelevant.[13]

3. *Some commissions, faced with a legacy of tariffs that fell far short of covering costs, were understandably reluctant to take the politically explosive step of a raising tariffs to cost-recovering levels.* Many developing or former socialist countries start their reforms with a large gap between revenues and costs. When the gap is large, it is totally unrealistic to expect that a new regulatory commission will be able to close the gap under the guise of making technical tariff adjustments, especially when political authorities have been hiding from the gap for many years. When faced with such a difficult and politically sensitive situation, a regulatory commission can almost always find creative but plausible reasons to rationalize small or no increases in tariffs. One common justification is that there are "insufficient data" to justify higher tariffs. Another is that the company could make a reasonable profit if it just met efficiency targets set by the regulator (usually ignoring, as in Orissa, that the targets have been set at impossibly high levels). To be fair to the regulators, many private companies have shown disappointing early progress in improving performance, though this sometimes can be explained by a government's unwillingness or inability to provide basic "law and order." For example, it appears that private companies in Georgia, India and South Africa often have no support and sometimes active opposition from the local police when they try to collect non-paying customers or illegally connected customers.[14] So even if the private distribution company has the approval of the regulator to charge tariffs that recover costs, this does not do much good if it cannot collect what it bills.

In 1993 the Bank was probably naïve in believing that it would be possible to create a regulatory system that would be fair to both investors and consumers by creating a new regulatory institution with nothing more than the formal elements of independence.[15] This "technocratic and legal" model of regulation ignores the fundamental reality that raising tariffs for retail customers is a politically charged exercise in the Bank's client countries—usually low-income countries whose existing electricity tariffs often fall far short of covering costs.

In such countries, almost everyone views an independent regulatory system with fear and trepidation. Ministers fear that a genuinely independent, regulatory commission may raise tariffs too quickly—possibly leading to political attacks from the opposition, riots and even the collapse

---

12. La Paz, "Tariffs Are Frozen Until January," *La Paz Bolivia*, November 1, 2001. In February 2002, the presidential decree was found to be unconstitutional by the Bolivian Constitutional Tribunal. The tribunal, which consists of six members selected by the Bolivian congress, is responsible for hearing formal complaints that a Bolivian government official or agency has overstepped its legal authority. Some observers have described the tribunal's decision as a landmark decision in Bolivia's efforts to create a credible "rule of law."

13. This would also appear to be true in Chile and Uruguay, where the legal norm is that "the commission proposes but the minister approves." But knowledgeable practitioners have observed that in these two countries it is politically difficult for a minister to overturn a commission decision if it is well-reasoned, well-documented, and well-publicized. Of course, there is nothing to prevent a minister from calling the head of the commission and indicate a strong preference for a technical study that produces lower rather higher numbers. This was particularly easy to do in Chile, where the head of the commission was also the Minister of Economy.

14. Letter from AES Orissa Distribution Private Limited to Chief Secretary, Government of Orissa, July 25, 2001 and Washington Post, "For South Africa's Poor: A New Power Struggle," November 6, 2001 p. A-1.

15. The formal elements of independence include: clear mandate excluding ministerial discretion established in law; appointed on the basis of professional criteria with restrictions on conflict of interest; protected from arbitrary removal during fixed terms; staggered terms that do not coincide with the election cycle; and earmarked funding. See Smith (1997).

of the government.[16] Investors fear the opposite. They are fearful that a new regulatory commission will not have the courage to raise tariffs quickly enough so that they can recover their costs and earn a profit. They are also afraid that, once they make their investments, they run the risk of being held hostage to a form of *de facto* expropriation through unfavorable regulatory decisions. Finally, the new regulators themselves are also afraid. They are fearful that they will be blamed for the regulatory equivalent of the "perfect storm"—significant increases in retail tariffs, no obvious improvements in quality of service and highly visible profits for a new private company that is largely owned by foreigners. All of these conflicting fears make it almost impossible for a new regulatory system to be a technical and legal exercise in the first years of its existence.

---

16. "Four Die As Andhra Police Open Fire on Protesters," *The Times of India News Service*, August 29, 2000; and "Indian Protesters Burn World Bank Chief In Effigy," *Dow Jones Newswire*, November 11, 2000. However, government ministers sometimes want higher tariffs. It was recently reported that several ministers in Brazil and Colombia were unhappy with their electricity regulators for keeping retail tariffs too low. The ministers believed that low tariffs would hurt the country's ability to attract foreign investment. They accused their regulators of failing to see the "big picture."

CHAPTER 3

REGULATION BY CONTRACT

In framing a government to be administered by men over men, the great difficulty lies in this: you must first enable the government to control the governed; and in the next place oblige it to control itself.

—James Madison, 1787

A good regulator is a boring regulator.

—U.S. power company official, 2002

What Is Regulation by Contract?

Two Definitions

Some observers have recommended *regulation by contract* as an alternative to regulatory independence. The essence of regulation by contract is pre-specification, in one or more formal or explicit agreements, of the formulas that determine prices that a distribution company is allowed to charge for the electricity it sells. This does *not* mean that the actual prices are pre-specified. What is pre-specified is the regulatory *treatment* (such as indexing, automatic pass-through or case-by-case determination) for the individual cost elements that together determine the retail tariff. The agreements are between the government and the private company.[17]

---

17. The U.S. power sector has operated under an informal understanding known as the "regulatory compact." The essence of the compact was that privately owned utilities would be allowed to recover "prudently incurred" operating and capital costs in return for assuming the obligation to meet all the electricity needs, upon demand, in their service areas. The compact was not written down in any one document. Instead, it was presumed to exist (at least by the private companies) in numerous regulatory practices, approvals, court cases and explicit or implicit understandings. In the late 1990s, a major controversy arose when the private companies argued that under the "regulatory compact" they were entitled to recover stranded costs when the government decided to introduce retail competition. For arguments in favor of this position, see Baumol et al. (1996); for a contrary view, see Michaels (1996). The fact that the two sides could not even agree as to whether a "regulatory compact" even existed suggests that this is not a workable model for developing countries.

The application of this general concept has yielded at least two different operational definitions. One definition of regulation by contract is that it is *regulation without a regulator.*[18] Under this definition, the regulatory contract is totally self-contained and self-administered like a commercial contract. Any disputes arising over implementation are handled by a regular court, an administrative court or a special expert panel. This is an appealing concept because it seems to offer the possibility of putting regulation on autopilot and eliminates the need to create a new regulatory entity.

A second definition is that regulation by contract is a detailed tariff-setting agreement administered by an independent regulator. Under this definition, *the regulatory contract does not replace the regulator but substantially limits the regulator's discretion.* In particular, it forces the regulator to set tariffs based on specific formulas rather than just general principles.

We use the second definition in this paper because we are not aware of any developing countries where the behavior of a privatized electricity distribution company is completely controlled by a regulatory contract with no further intervention by a government or regulatory entity. "Regulation without a regulator" does exist in the French water sector but the conditions that make it possible in France are not likely to be replicable in other countries, especially in developing or former socialist countries. (See Box 1.)

There seem to be four principal reasons why regulatory contracts for electricity distribution companies require continued administration by some government entity:

1. Most countries find it politically impossible to allow a company to calculate periodic price adjustments permitted by a tariff formula without further government oversight. In any democratic country, a government that accepted such an arrangement would be strongly criticized for abdicating its responsibilities to protect captive customers.[19] It would be especially dangerous if the company is foreign owned.
2. The values of key parameters of the tariff-setting formula, such as loss targets and power purchase pass-through mechanisms, need to be reset every several years. In general, courts have neither the technical expertise nor the inclination to do this. Therefore, the government must designate some governmental entity, other than the courts, to administer the contract and reset new values at the end of the tariff period.
3. Even with detailed rules, certain regulatory tasks will still need to be performed. These include applying indexing formulas, monitoring the distribution company's behavior with respect to pricing and quality of service, and making decisions about noncompliance and possible penalties.
4. Even if distribution tariff setting is susceptible to detailed specification, there are many other regulatory decisions that simply cannot be specified in advance. This is especially true if the power sector reform includes the phase-in of one or more forms of wholesale and retail competition which, in turn, will trigger the need to decide on the price and non-price terms of unbundled distribution and transmission access, obligations for back-up supply, and assessments of the degree of competitiveness in newly opened markets (i.e., market monitoring). Because a regulator is likely to be needed for these other decisions, it is probably more efficient for the same entity also to administer the regulatory contract for distribution tariff setting.

---

18. In referring to long-term concession or leasing arrangements, the World Bank's 1994 *World Development Report* stated that "these arrangements....do not require the establishment of independent regulatory bodies because regulatory procedures [and regulatory provisions in general] are specified in the underlying contract" (p.10). Alternatively, if there is a regulator, it is limited to functioning as a "contract monitoring office."

19. *Captive customers* are those who lack access to alternative suppliers and cannot generate electricity at their own facilities at competitive prices.

Box 1: THE FRENCH WATER SECTOR: REGULATION WITHOUT A REGULATOR

The French water sector has operated for many years under regulatory contracts without a regulator. Under this system, implemented through hundreds of municipally granted concessions or leases, private companies provide about 80 percent of the water supply and about 45 percent of the sewage services.

However, a recent, in-depth study of the sector (Shugart, 1998) suggests that the combination of conditions that make it possible to have regulation without a regulator in France are *not likely to be replicable* in electricity distribution in developing countries for the foreseeable future. These conditions include the following:

- **Model contracts.** The Ministry of Interior has developed model concessions and leases that are widely used by municipalities. Experienced central government officials are available to assist municipal officials in developing and implementing these contracts for local circumstances.
- **Well-developed case law and legal doctrines.** More than 200 years of highly developed case law and legal doctrines inform the implementation of concessions and leases. In particular, there are well-defined procedures and standards for dealing with three problem areas: actions taken by a public authority that raise the costs of a concessionaire (*fait du prince*), unexpected material conditions that make construction or operations more costly (*sujétions imprévues*) and temporary difficulties typically brought on by the increase in the price of an input that clearly exceed any levels expected at the time the contract was signed (*imprévision*).
- **A respected appellate tribunal.** Disputes over implementation of the concessions and leases are handled by an experienced and knowledgeable appellate court known as the Conseil d'Etat, which functions as a special administrative tribunal. Unlike its Anglo-Saxon counterparts, the Conseil d'Etat has the authority to make decisions on both substance and process. In this sense, it acts as a "shadow regulator."
- **Private operators are French companies.** The sector is dominated by two large French companies. They are sensitive to "reputational concerns." Moreover, the fact that they are well-known French companies also eliminates any sensitivity about payments to foreign companies.
- **Common educational backgrounds.** Many of the executives in the private companies and the high level civil servants in the relevant ministries attended the same elite educational institutions (*grandes écoles*). This produces a sense of "professional honor" and a commitment to the successful delegation of a public service.
- **Cultural traditions.** The principle of moderation is well developed in French society, and excessive argumentativeness is considered "vulgar."

In light of these considerations, it is reasonable to expect that some government entity will need to administer the regulatory contract.

Key Characteristics

Experience in Latin America and elsewhere suggests that the terms *regulation by contract* and *regulatory contract* be defined as one or more written agreements between a private distribution company and a government that have the following features:[20]

- The government pre-commits to a specified regulatory system that establishes how retail tariffs will be set for a multi-year period typically ranging from four to eight years. In most instances, it is the government rather than the regulator that designs the regulatory system.

---

20. Our focus in this paper is on regulation by contract for the principal distribution supplier. Equally important to power sector reform, but beyond the scope of this paper, are the issues involved in regulating off-grid and mini-grid suppliers.

- The regulatory contract is specified prior to receiving privatization bids so that bidders can estimate their likely future stream of revenues.
- Even though the government usually designs the tariff system and makes the formal commitment, a separate and possibly independent regulatory entity will implement the contract.
- The agreement contains a formula with pre-specified parameters that determine how annual total revenue or average tariff levels will be established by the regulator. The formula will often distinguish between controllable and non-controllable input costs. Controllable costs will be tied to external indices or benchmarks with performance targets and associated rewards and penalties. Non-controllable costs will be automatically passed through on a regular or episodic basis.[21]
- The contract will usually specify some process for dealing with unforeseen events that can have a significant effect on the utility's costs or revenues. These might include damage from severe storms and major changes in taxes, duties and environmental regulations.
- The regulatory contract may have an indefinite life but with scheduled revisions every four to eight years.
- In the first multi-year tariff-setting period, the regulator will administer the terms of a tariff formula over which it has little or no discretion. In later tariff-setting periods, the regulator will have more discretion over selecting the values of some of the parameters in the formula.
- The contract will usually specify three types of regulatory actions: resetting of the parameters of the tariff formula at the end of the multi-year period; periodic adjustments for inflation or "true-up" for the difference between actual and projected values; and extraordinary adjustments for unexpected or difficult to predict events that could have a significant effect on the financial condition of the distribution company.
- The agreement will usually build on a pre-privatization "clean-up" of the public enterprise's balance sheet.
- The agreement may be a stand-alone document such as a license or concession. But more typically it will be embedded within or derived from a privatization agreement, secondary regulations or decrees or the power sector reform law. In these latter cases, regulation by contract is not a single agreement but rather a combination of concessions, licenses, decrees and laws. The regulatory system will not be sustainable unless the documents are consistent.
- The agreement may specify that disputes between the regulator and the company will be settled through normal judicial channels such as the country's existing court system, through a specialized non-judicial channel such as an arbitration panel (within country or external), or through a special electricity appellate court or an appellate body that hears appeals of the decisions of all infrastructure regulators.
- If the gap between revenues and costs is large, the government will have to commit to a subsidy program. The subsidies can take different forms: direct subsidies to the distribution company (such as a subsidized price for the power that the distribution company pays for bulk purchases), tariff subsidies to poor customers, and capital cost subsidies to connect new rural customers.[22]

---

21. The extent of the pass through for a non-controllable cost is usually based on an assessment of whether the price, quantity or both elements of the input cost are beyond the control of the distribution utility. (See Box 4.)

22. Subsidies that are tied to output performance have been described as "output-based aid." For descriptions of how such programs could be applied in electricity, see www.rru.worldbank.org.

What Government Entity Should Administer the Contract?

In the preceding list of characteristics, it is assumed that government will create the regulatory contract, but that implementation and enforcement of the contract will be transferred to an independent regulatory entity. Why should there be this split of functions?

The initial decision to privatize and set up a viable regulatory system that will support privatization must be a government decision because it inherently *a political act*. When the initial gap between costs and revenues is large (as is often the case in developing countries), the decision to privatize requires more political courage than technical expertise. Therefore, it would be unreasonable and naïve to try to delegate this fundamental political decision to a group of technical experts residing in a newly created regulatory commission.

Once the political decision has been made, however, it has a better chance of surviving if implementation can be handed over to a regulatory entity that is insulated from ongoing short-term political pressures. After the contract is in place, it is more likely to be administered in a fair and impartial way by an independent regulator than by a new minister who probably was not a member of the government that negotiated the contract.

Power Purchase Agreements: a Useful Precedent?

Some private investors have argued that there already exists a working model in the power sector for regulation by contract. In their view, the numerous power purchase agreements (PPAs) signed in many developing countries represent a regulatory model that could be replicated in distribution. PPAs usually take the form of direct bilateral contracts between a private investor and a government entity. From the perspective of the private investor, the single most appealing feature of a PPA is that it specifies a formula that determines how prices will be established over a 10-to-25 year period. Because the pricing formula is "locked in" for the life of the contract, there is no need to come back to the regulator every year for a new tariff decision. In fact, the regulator may never have reviewed the PPA and may be legally precluded from modifying its terms once the contract is signed.

Although investors almost always like PPAs because they reduce risk and help to ensure profitability, many governments have had second thoughts about the PPAs that they or previous governments have signed. Their principal criticism is that the prices are too high and too much risk has been transferred to final customers. They point out that many of the PPAs were negotiated without any attempt at competitive procurement. In Guatemala, the Dominican Republic, the Philippines and Pakistan, new governments (or opposition parties) have contended that the pricing formulas in existing PPAs may reflect corruption or incompetence.[23] It has also been pointed out the structure of many PPAs, particularly the requirement to take power even if means foregoing a lower cost supply source, makes PPAs an impediment to creating organized bulk power markets (Woolf and Halpern, 2001).

Apart from these criticisms, there is also the reality that the basic characteristics of distribution make it harder to design and implement a regulatory contract in distribution than in generation. (See Table 1 for a listing of some key differences between distribution and generation.) Three characteristics in particular make regulatory contracts in distribution more difficult to negotiate and sustain than PPAs: the large number of customers, the high visibility of the retail

---

23. Similar allegations of corruption in the awarding of French water concessions led to the passage of an "Anti-Corruption Law" in 1994. The law establishes a transparent multi-step process for selection of concessionaires. Its key requirements are *"openness* (the municipality must publish a notice of its intention to delegate a public service and then review the qualifications of the respondents in order to select a short-list), *competition* (presentation of fully developed proposals by more than one firm), and *transparency* (presentation of various reports to the municipal assembly explaining the conclusions reached)." See Shugart (1998), p. 104. The Shugart dissertation contains one of the best descriptions of the French concession system currently available in English.

TABLE 1: REGULATION BY CONTRACT: GENERATION VERSUS DISTRIBUTION

Characteristic	Generation	Distribution
Parties to the contract	Private investor and government as a buyer	Private investor and government as a regulator
Number of customers	One, usually a state-owned enterprise	Thousands of customers
Price visibility	Low (at least initially)	High
Investment	One time	Ongoing
Quality of service	One-dimensional (i.e. availability) and relatively easy to measure	Multi-dimensional and hard to measure
Scheduled resetting of tariff parameters	Usually none	Every four to seven years
Regulators role in designing contract	Limited to non-existent	Limited to non-existent
Economic problems	Exposure to foreign exchange fluctuations Price may be too high because of corruption or incompetence in procurement	Exposure to foreign exchange fluctuations

price and the need for ongoing investments. Despite these characteristics, however, we think that regulatory contracts for electricity distribution can and should be negotiated. In Chapters 5 and 6, we discuss some specific features of sustainable regulatory contracts.

Is a Regulatory Contract Different from a Commercial Contract?

When most people think of contracts, they think of *commercial contracts*. In a normal commercial contract, one party is a seller and the other is a buyer. The seller provides a product or service in return for a payment from the buyer. A privatization agreement is like a traditional commercial contract. The government is selling some or all of the ownership rights to an existing distribution entity and a private company is the buyer.

A regulatory contract bears some resemblance to a commercial contract in that it is based on a *quid pro quo*. The essence of a regulatory contract is that the government agrees to commit itself (or a regulatory commission that it will create) to implement a pre-specified tariff-setting system to provide a reasonably high degree of certainty as to the company's future revenues over a multi-year period. In return, the private company agrees to provide electricity distribution service with certain quality attributes to specified customers over a defined period of time. The rationale for bringing the two contracts together—the privatization contract and the regulatory contract—is that no serious and reputable private company would be willing to buy distribution assets unless it knows the services that it will be obligated to provide and the prices that it will be allowed to charge.

However, a regulatory contract is clearly different from a normal commercial contract in several important respects. First, one of the parties to the contract, the government, is performing two roles. It is the seller or lessor of the assets, and it is also the enforcer of the regulatory contract. Second, there are asymmetric rights in the contract. In normal commercial contracts, there is a balance of rights between the two parties. In a regulatory contract, the government usually reserves some extra-contractual rights for itself. For example, it may reserve the right to an early termination, the right to make unilateral amendments to the contract and the right to prohibit early terminations of the contract by the private party. These are the traditional rights of a government when it is authorizes a private company to perform a public service. Nevertheless, if the regulatory contract is to be credible, the government that signs the contract must somehow convince potential investors that it will impose restrictions on the ability of future governments to exercise these rights. In summary, the two distingushing elements of regulation by contract are that a government pre-commits to a fairly specific form of tariff setting and also agrees to limit its own ability to modify the tariff-setting system for a specified number of years.

Most investors would prefer that the regulatory contract be viewed as a simply a contract between them and the government. This is a naïve view, because regulation by contract does not take place in a vacuum. Although regulation by contract has developed primarily to attract investment, it will not be sustainable if it focuses exclusively on this one goal. Regulation by contract must achieve two goals: it must (1) protect consumers from monopoly prices and inferior quality of service while also (2) attracting investors who will make the investments to provide the service at affordable prices. The objective of regulation by contract is to have the best of both worlds and to define the trade-offs between these two conflicting regulatory objectives. The idea is to limit the discretion of the regulator in areas that are known to deter investment while at the same time using independent regulation to avoid uncertainties for investor created by political micro-management and changes of government or governmental policy.

Should Regulation by Contract Be Just a Transition Mechanism?

It has been suggested that regulation by contract is needed only to launch the privatization process (that is the first, multi-year tariff period after privatization). In other words, it is a technique for "jump-starting" the regulatory and privatization process. The rationale for limiting regulation by contract to just this transition period is that this is the period when the contract is most needed: the new regulatory commission is inexperienced, will not have a "track record" and is operating in a "weak governance environment." (The is a polite way of saying that the commission may be formally independent but neither the commission nor the government can be trusted with much discretion over tariffs.) Although these are plausible justifications for using regulation by contract in developing countries, it is interesting that regulation by contract has also become the regulatory system of choice in many developed countries that are *not* operating in weak governance environments.

In many developed countries, multi-year price or revenue caps, which are a form of regulation by contract, have become the system of choice in setting retail tariffs both for new regulatory commissions, such as exist in England and Wales and the Netherlands, and old regulatory commissions, such as exist in the United States. It appears that these countries have decided to commit themselves to a multi-year (as opposed to an annual) tariff-setting system because they have concluded that a multi-year tariff system embedded within a formal regulatory contract provides stronger incentives for the regulated enterprise to be efficient. In effect, they have decided to give up regulatory discretion because they expect that they will get more efficient performance from the regulated entity if they commit to a multi-year tariff regime. The U.S. example is particularly interesting because none of the U.S. commissions that chose to adopt multi-year tariff-setting systems were legally obligated to do so. In general, most U.S. commissions have operated for many years under very general laws that simply say that the commissions should set tariffs that are "just and reasonable" and "not unduly discriminatory." Nevertheless, some U.S. commissions have chosen to restrict their own flexibility and commit themselves to a multi-year tariff-setting system because they concluded that it was a better system for consumers. This suggests that a performance-based, multi-year tariff-setting system, the key component of the regulatory contract, should be the preferred approach for regulating private distribution entities in developing and developed countries and not just for a transition period.

CHAPTER 4

REAL-WORLD REGULATORY EXPERIENCES: BRAZIL AND INDIA

Regulation by Contract: The Latin American Approach

The most prominent example of regulation by contract in developing countries can be found in the more than 60 distribution privatizations that have occurred throughout Latin America over the last 15 years.[24] In general, the regulatory component of these privatizations is a pre-specified tariff-setting formula, with fixed parameters, that is used to set the distribution company's average retail price or overall revenue over a multi-year period.[25] Typically, the formula provides for automatic pass-through of non-controllable costs and benchmarking or indexing of controllable costs. To provide additional comfort to investors, the tariff-setting formula is often written into a law, the concession or privatization agreement, commission orders, or sometimes in all of these legal documents. Under this standard Latin American approach, the regulator's initial role is

---

24. Management contracts could also be viewed as a form of regulation by contract. Management contracts are typically used when a government is unwilling to privatize or a private investor is unwilling to invest capital in a state-owned enterprise. As a lesser alternative to full privatization, the government may write a contract with the private company so that the company assumes responsibility for general management or one or more operating functions such as meter reading, billing, collection and maintenance. In Africa, management contracts have been recommended as a necessary prerequisite (i.e., a cleanup mechanism) if there is to be any possibility of privatization. Those who make this recommendation are arguing that a company needs to be an operator first in order to be an investor later (Block 1998). Such contracts are often difficult to write and implement because they require careful delineation of the responsibilities of the government and private company. It has been argued that a management contract is harder to write than a full privatization agreement. A 1994 survey of management contracts in electricity and other infrastructure sectors found that generally they were not successful (World Bank 1995).

25. To be more precise, the formula is for the "distribution margin," that is, the capital and operating costs associated with the movement of electricity over distribution lines and commercialization activities. In addition to the distribution margin, there is usually some pre-specified benchmark for the pass through of power-purchase costs. See Chapter 5 under "Passing-Through the Cost of Power Purchases".

quite limited. For the first tariff-setting period, usually four to eight years, the regulator essentially administers a formula that was written by someone else. The regulator functions, in effect, like a referee at a soccer game: rather than writing the rules, he simply enforces them.

The Special Case of Brazil

Brazil's approach to regulation by contract is both similar to and different from other Latin American countries. It is similar in that Brazil, like the rest of Latin America, uses concession agreements. It is different in that Brazilian concession contracts for power distribution are essentially "stand-alone" regulatory contracts between the granting federal or state government and the private company that becomes the concessionaire. In contrast, the key elements of distribution concessions in other Latin American countries are typically tied to fairly detailed tariff-setting formulas specified in comprehensive power sector reform law.

Although a similar tariff-setting system was recommended for Brazil by the government's privatization and restructuring consultants, the country went ahead with privatization and restructuring without the benefit of a general power sector reform law. It appears that such a law was never passed in Brazil because of the country's inability to reach political agreement on a reform "game plan." As a result, the executive branch of the Brazilian government was forced to pursue major reforms while relying on a "patchwork" of concession agreements and regulations that emphasize "principles" rather than "details," while hoping that more-detailed secondary legislation would be drafted latter.[26] One Brazilian consultant has observed that Brazil's "original sin" was that "the plane took off even though we hadn't finished all of the design work and there was still some welding to be done."

Initially, the Brazilian approach of regulation through stand-alone concession contracts—a system that gives the regulator considerable discretion in applying a general tariff formula—seemed to produce remarkable results, at least from the perspective of investment bankers. By the time ANEEL, the new national electricity regulator, was created in 1997, ten distribution companies had already been sold via concession contracts for a total of US$12 billion dollars (Araujo, 2001). The average price of US$1,400 per customer obtained by Brazil's distribution privatizations beat all previous world records. AES paid a 93 percent premium to acquire CEEE in October 1997 and Enron acquired Elektro at a 99 percent premium in July 1998. In less than five years, private investors invested more than US$27 billion in the Brazilian power sector. These impressive results may reflect the fact that the Brazilian privatization was, in most instances, led by BNDES, the state-owned privatization bank, which may have been more interested in maximizing privatization revenues than in creating a workable and sustainable power sector. It may also reflect a perception on the part of investors that they would be able to "game" the regulatory system.

Now, with the benefit of hindsight, some of the hidden weaknesses in the Brazilian regulatory model have surfaced as the stand-alone concession system has been subjected to major macroeconomic and natural shocks. In 1999 the country had to confront a 56 percent devaluation of its currency. In 2000, the MAE (the wholesale energy market) was not able to go operational because of several legal and technical problems. In 2001, a severe drought forced the government to mandate a country-wide electricity rationing program. These major shocks produced disputes over interpretation of various concessions, contracts, regulations and laws. Without the reference point of a single electricity-law-of-the-land and detailed tariff-setting provisions, there have been frequent disagreements as to which of several legal provisions took precedence. By the end of 2001, what may have seemed to be a very successful, ad hoc web of regulation-by-contracts

---

26. One private power executive recently observed that the Brazilian power sector "is currently governed by dozens of laws, resolutions, decrees and regulations." As quoted in "Enertrade calls for a new private sector law—Brazil," *Bnamericas,* January 16, 2002.

seemed to collapse. In 2002 the Brazilian government proposed a series of 33 major policy initiatives characterized as "mid-course" corrections. It remains to be seen whether Brazil's new government will pursue these changes—and if it does, whether the changes will produce clarity and consistency or just create new complexities and inconsistencies.[27]

What Went Wrong in Brazil?

Because other Latin American countries have generally had success with regulation by contract, it is worth taking a closer look at why Brazil is now encountering major regulatory and economic problems with its particular approach. The Brazilian experience provides some lessons on "what not to do" with regulatory contracts.

Vagueness in Tariff-Setting Provisions

The tariff provisions in most Brazilian concession contracts cover only the initial tariff-setting period. Even for that period, however, some key terms are not clearly defined. For example, a typical agreement will give a distribution company the right to petition ANEEL for "extraordinary" tariff adjustments if such adjustments are needed to maintain "economic-financial equilibrium."[28] Yet, the concept is so vague and subjective that no distribution company has ever succeeded in getting such an adjustment.

The concession agreements are even more vague about what happens at the end of the first multi-year tariff period. The concession agreements make a general reference to the "repositioning" of tariffs at the end of the tariff period. The guidance as to what repositioning means is typically limited to a single sentence that states that the regulator:

> shall process the revision of the amounts of rates for commercialization of power, altering them upwards or downwards, taking into account the cost of and market structures of the Concessionaire, the levels of rates charged by similar companies in the nationwide and international context, stimuli for efficiency and for reasonableness of rates.[29]

As a consequence, ANEEL now finds itself in the difficult position of having to develop some basic rules and processes for setting tariffs more than five years after some of the distribution companies were created. This has led to bitter and unnecessary regulatory disputes that other Latin American countries have avoided.

Perhaps the most contentious issue is the calculation of the *regulatory asset base*—the amount of capital stock that the regulator uses to calculate the overall revenue to be recovered in retail tariffs. Like most Latin American countries, no value was specified for the regulatory asset base at the time of privatization. Unlike other Latin American countries, Brazil also did not specify a *methodology* for calculating the regulatory asset base at the end of the first multi-year tariff period. As the first tariff period came to a close for more than 50 distribution companies, the trade

27. Most of these proposals relate to market and tariff design issues. For a perceptive assessment of second generation of regulatory governance and other institutional issues, see Brown and de Paula (2002).

28. See *Concession Agreement of ElectroPaulo*, Clause 7, Sub-clause 2. Although many lengthy articles have been written about the meaning of the concept, there is no generally accepted operational definition. The concept of an "economic-financial equilibrium" comes out of the French concession tradition. Although Brazil adopted the concept, it did not adopt the more than 100 years of the French case law that gives operational meaning to the concept. The regulatory contracts in many Anglo-Saxon countries use a different approach. Rather than referring to a general concept, they often refer to a "z" factor that is usually defined in terms of specific events (such as damage caused by extreme weather conditions or changes in tax codes and environmental regulations) that provide the distribution company with a right to petition the regulator for an extraordinary tariff adjustment.

29. *Distribution Concession Agreement No 12/97*, AES Sul, Article 7, Sub-Article 6. It appears that the concession agreements in Colombia are also vague. See Mercados Energeticos (2002).

association of Brazilian distribution companies proposed a methodology that would produce a regulatory asset base with a value that appeared to be two to three times larger than the value that would result from the regulator's proposed methodology. Because the dispute was so contentious, the President of Brazil found it necessary to appoint a special inter-ministerial task force to try to resolve the dispute at the worst of all times—a few weeks before the country's presidential elections.

Brazil could have avoided this unnecessary regulatory battle if it had simply followed the approach of other Latin American countries, which was to specify, prior to privatization, a methodology for calculating the regulatory asset base for both the initial and later tariff-setting periods.[30] If it had followed this precedent, the debate would have been limited to the details of applying the methodology rather than having to grapple with the threshold issue of which methodology should be used in the first place.[31]

Uncertainty about Pass-Through for Power-Purchase Costs

Even in the initial period, the details of the mechanism for passing power-purchase costs through to retail customers were not well developed. The concession contracts typically make reference to a general formula that has a component A for "non-controllable "costs"—mainly power-purchase costs—and a component B for "controllable costs"—principally distribution O&M costs. But ANEEL did not develop detailed rules for the pass-through of power-purchase costs until after most of the privatizations had occurred. ANEEL's rules establish *valores normativos* (VNs), which are indexed fuel and technology specific caps on the level of power-purchase costs that distribution companies can pass through to their captive customers.[32] The specific rules for indexation of these VN costs have been clarified or amended four times since the system was created in August 1998. In contrast, the rules for power-purchase cost pass-through have been more stable in other Latin American countries (Argentina, Bolivia and Chile) even though they may create other problems.[33]

Low Allowed Prices for Pass-Through of Power-Purchase Costs

Potential investors in new thermal generating plants have complained that because the administratively established VN levels for this type of plant reflect a very low return on assets, they are not economically viable. In theory, although a Brazilian distribution company could pay more than the specified VN, ANEEL's regulations would prohibit it from passing through to its retail customers any costs exceeding 1.05 times the VN value. It is not surprising, then, that Brazilian

---

30. For example, the primary or secondary laws in Chile, Colombia, Peru and Uruguay specify that the allowed capital costs of a distribution utility must be based on the capital costs of a "model efficient firm" which is a type of reproduction cost calculation that has now become fairly well-defined in these countries. (See Rudnick and Donoso, 2000). In contrast, Brazilian laws and concession agreements are silent on the calculation of this key cost component of tariffs. ANEEL has also proposed a type of reproduction cost calculation. However, ANEEL would perform the replacement cost calculation on an asset-by-asset basis, whereas the other Latin American regulators use a generalized model to calculate reproduction cost. The problem with the ANEEL proposal is that it requires large amounts of data and is costly and time-consuming for the company to calculate and for ANEEL to review. In February 2003 ANEEL issued technical notes that strongly suggest that it move to the "model efficient firm" approach used almost everywhere else in Latin America. A major, but not widely appreciated, advantage of this approach is that it greatly reduces "information asymmetry" between the company and the regulator. Distribution companies tend to reveal considerable detailed information about their operations and costs when asked to comment on the accuracy of the model-efficient-firm calculation when it is applied to their circumstances.

31. A discussion of the pros and cons of using different methodologies for setting regulatory asset base is beyond the scope of this paper. See Alexander (2001). For an overview of different approaches by different British regulators, see Carne et al. (1999). The consensus among most experts is that the selected method must be consistently applied once it is selected.

32. ANEEL, Resolution 233/99, July 29, 1999.

33. See for example Article 49 (Nodal Prices) of the Bolivian Electricity Law. See also the discussion in Chapter 5 under "Passing-Through the Cost of Power Purchases".

distributors have been reluctant to sign long-term power purchase agreements (PPAs) with generators for new thermal-fired plants. Such PPAs are needed for financing new generation projects in the absence of a workable spot energy market. To address this issue, in February 2002 the Brazilian government announced a power sector reform program that includes a proposal to allow future VNs to be determined by market auctions rather than through the administrative calculations of a regulator. The new Lula government, which came to power in January 2003, will have to decide whether or not to adopt this policy.

Foreign Exchange Risk

Potential thermoelectric investors have also been concerned about what has been referred to as the "dollar-cost/real-revenue mismatch." The cost structure for proposed thermoelectric plants in Brazil almost always requires significant expenditures in U.S. dollars. With fuel costs, project debt, return on equity, and EPC (engineering, procurement and construction) costs denominated in U.S. dollars, a gas-fired plant will typically incur about 80 percent of its costs in dollars. In the VN formulas, the weights for dollar versus local currency costs are subject to a case-by-case determination by ANEEL. Although the Brazilian government enacted special legislation to reduce this uncertainty, the new law applies only for a limited number of years and to a limited number of emergency thermal plants on a government-approved list.

In contrast, the exchange rate pass-through provisions of other Southern Cone countries[34] are usually specified in their respective Electricity Laws and therefore control the provisions in concession contracts.[35] In these countries, investors face little or no uncertainty and, if there is less than complete pass-through, they can reflect this risk in their offered prices—an option that is not available to generators in Brazil because of the VN ceilings.

Uncertainty in the Legal Framework

As discussed earlier, Brazil, unlike its neighbors, has a patchwork of laws, resolutions, regulations and concession agreements. It is not always clear how they relate to each other and which takes precedence when they are inconsistent. The regulatory framework was never consolidated into a single national electricity law, as was envisioned when the power sector reform was initiated.

The problem of inconsistency recently arose in what has been referred to the as the "Annex V dispute." This dispute was triggered by a major drought in the second half of 2001. To prevent rolling blackouts and brownouts, the government ordered a mandatory 20 percent cut in power consumption across most of the country. This in turn produced claims by distributors that they were entitled to compensation (mostly from government-owned generators) for the lower revenues produced by the government-mandated rationing. The generators, in the final turn, claimed that that they were not required to make such payments because the rationing was triggered by a "force majeure."

Much of the dispute revolved around conflicting definitions of "force majeure" found in different laws, presidential resolutions and concession agreements. Because somewhere between US$2 billion and 4 billion was at stake, the disputing parties were willing to spend millions of dollars on lawyers to protect their claims before the dispute was finally resolved in a wide-ranging settlement in December 2001. Despite this agreement and subsequent discussions, full payment of the settlement amounts has not occurred as of this writing (early 2003). Other Southern Cone countries appear to be less vulnerable to this type of dispute because their concession agreements are embedded in reasonably well-defined and consistent hierarchies of laws and contracts.

A recent multi-sector study of Latin American concessions found that the extent of "legal coverage" clearly affects the likelihood that the regulatory contract will be sustainable. In a survey of 713 Latin American concessions in infrastructure industries (water, transport, telecom and energy),

---

34. The "Southern Cone" countries of Latin America are Argentina, Brazil, Chile, Paraguay, and Uruguay.
35. See, for example, the secondary legislation of Bolivia, which went into effect on the same day as the primary legislation (Government of Bolivia, *Regulations for Prices and Tariffs*, December 21, 1994, Article 18).

the probability of renegotiation of the concession agreement was determined to be 18 percent if the regulatory framework is in law, 48 percent if it is in a decree and 61 percent if it is just in a contract and concession (Guasch, 2000). When the regulatory framework is in law, it is almost always in a decree and a contract or concession as well. Presumably, this triple coverage gives comfort to investors and makes it less likely that the government will try to renege on the agreement. Also, when the regulatory contract is clearly derived from a national law, there is a smaller likelihood of inconsistencies that can lead to later legal battles.

Lack of Respect for Contracts

All of this suggests that regulation by contract is not likely to be sustainable unless it is embedded in a reasonably consistent legal framework that reflects a generally consensual vision of the new structure. But this is a necessary but not sufficient condition. The legal system could be designed to be as "tight as a glove" but it will still fail if the substantive elements of the contract mandate actions or impose requirements that are not commercially viable.

Moreover, although the contract could be well written, it could just as well be a "work of fiction" if there is a tradition of not honoring contracts. There are no hard statistics, but some knowledgeable observers have claimed that there is a tradition of not honoring contracts within the Brazilian power sector (Maurer, 2001). This was seen most recently in the aftermath of the 2001 rationing disputes. Those power enterprises that owed money had a strong economic incentive not to pay their creditors. The incentive exists, in part, because Brazilian courts are slower in making decisions than courts in other Latin American countries. It is not uncommon for Brazilian courts to take five or more years to resolve major commercial disputes. And when the decision is finally resolved, there may be not be an inflation adjustment on the amount due. So the debtor has every incentive to delay payment and try to delay the judicial process because, even if it loses in court, it will benefit by paying much less when finally forced to honor the contract.

Regulation by Principles: The Case of India (So Far)

The regulatory system in India is quite different from the typical Latin American system. The first sub-national electricity commission in India was created in the state of Orissa. The other new Indian state electricity regulatory commissions, following the Orissa commission's lead, operate under a U.S.-style regulatory system, which means they are formally independent of the state governments. Unlike their Latin American counterparts, however, they currently administer a tariff-setting system that (1) is keyed to general principles, as opposed to a specific formula; and (2) is annual as opposed to multi-year tariff-setting.[36] In practice, this has meant that investors are forced to guess what the level of tariff increase will be in any given year. (See Table 2 for an overview of the regulatory models used in France, India, Latin America, the United Kingdom and the United States.)

Although the Indian regulatory system superficially resembles the U.S. system, it differs in three important respects. First, the new Indian regulators have uniformly interpreted their statutes to require that they must completely re-examine retail tariffs every year under a traditional (but flawed) cost-of-service tariff system.[37] In contrast, a U.S. regulatory commission will normally

---

36. For example, the Orissa Electricity Reform Act states that tariffs shall be "just and reasonable...[and] promote economic efficiency in the supply and consumption of electricity." The tariff-setting criteria in other countries are even more vague. For example, the Hungarian Law uses the term "justified costs" without giving a definition. Laws in Central and Eastern Europe use terms like "objectively determined" tariffs based on "rationalized" costs without definitions. See Stern and Davis (1999).

37. These include overoptimistic efficiency targets, less-than-full pass-through of non-controllable costs, and underestimates of cash working capital requirements. Generally, governments will often pressure government-owned power enterprises to project high efficiency improvements in their tariff filing because this justifies lower subsidy payments from the government or lower tariff increases for consumers. The government power enterprises will usually accede to the wishes of their owners even though they know that the efficiency improvement estimates are unrealistic.

TABLE 2: ALTERNATIVE REGULATORY MODELS

	France (water sector)	Latin America	Great Britain	United States	India
Separate Regulator?	No	Yes	Yes (national)	Yes (national and state)	Yes (national and state
Specifity of Regulatory Contract	Medium	High (Bolivia, Chile, Peru) Low (Brazil, Colombia)	High	Low (general principles interpreted in case law)	Low (general principles without case law)
Regulatory Decisions Reviewed by Special Appellate Tribunal?	Yes	No except for Bolivia	Yes (Competition Commission)	No	No, but proposed by government
Ownership of Regulated Entities	Private	Private and public (varies by country)	Mostly private	Mostly private	Mostly public
Form of Private Sector Participation	Concessions and leases	Concessions that are close to full privatization	Full privatization	Full privatization	Full privatization

review a company's tariffs only if the company or its customers complains to the commission. U.S. commissions are under no legal obligation to review retail tariffs every year. Therefore, companies such as Kentucky Utilities and Florida Power and Light have operated for many years without having to file new tariffs with their state regulatory commissions.

Second, with the exception of Orissa and Delhi, the new Indian regulators are regulating public rather than private entities.[38] When the regulated entity is government-owned, the regulator will usually find itself trying to move prices up to reflect costs.[39] Although state-owned power enterprises often desperately want to file for tariff increases, they are usually blocked from making such requests by government owners who fear that any tariff increases will antagonize voters. In contrast, the principal regulatory task in the United States, where about 75 percent of the sector is privately owned, is to get tariffs down to cost levels.

Third, state-owned Indian power enterprises generally ignore the directives of their regulators because the regulators have little or no ability to impose rewards and penalties on them. As one Indian regulator observed, "My orders are just pretty poetry."

---

38. Even though several Indian state power enterprises have now been "functionally unbundled" into separate government corporations, these new corporations still find themselves subject to substantial government control. In particular, they do not have control over the tariff applications that they file with the new state regulatory commissions. In the last two years, Indian state governments have ordered new power enterprises not to file tariff applications, to withdraw previously filed applications or to file tariff applications that do not recover their full costs. The former chairman of India's Central Electricity Regulatory Commission recently observed that "the regulated [state-owned] entities defy the commissions by non-compliance with tacit government approval." Rao (2001).

39. The Indian Ministry of Power estimates that revenues cover only 69 percent of costs for the average Indian distribution entity and this represents a decline from 80 percent.

Regulation by Contract: A Proposal For India

Several Indian states have announced their intention to privatize their state-owned distribution systems. To achieve this goal, the World Bank has recommended that Indian regulators move to a form of "regulation by contract" for potential private distribution companies that would be more akin to what exists in Latin America and elsewhere (Lim, 2001). In India, this new regulatory system is called "performance-based multi-year tariffs" or "medium-term tariff fixation." Like Latin America, the key elements of the proposed system are (1) automatic pass-through of cost elements that are largely beyond the distribution entity's control (such as power purchases and taxes) and (2) indexing and efficiency targets for cost elements that can be controlled (such as losses and labor costs). Numerous conferences and workshops have been held to discuss how multi-year tariffs might be implemented.[40] A newly proposed national electricity law seems to encourage its adoption. But even if Indian state electricity commissions were to replace their current annual cost-of-service system with a multi-year price or revenue cap system, there would still remain a major problem of regulatory credibility.

Is It Legal?

The problem of regulatory credibility arises because, under most current Indian proposals, multi-year tariffs would be *permitted* rather than *required*. This means that an existing Indian state regulatory commission would have to voluntarily give up its current legal right to revisit tariffs annually and commit itself to accepting a formula that specifies a tariff trajectory for several years. This raises the obvious question of whether an Indian state commission of 2002 can legally bind the commissions of 2003, 2004 and 2005, etc. to a particular tariff-setting regime and, more important, whether investors would believe such a commitment.

Given the current lack of a clear legal foundation for multi-year tariffs, it has been recommended that any Indian regulatory commission that decides to adopt multi-year tariffs must adopt a "belt and suspenders" approach to create the new system. This would involve putting the elements of the new tariff system in as many commission documents (policy statements, tariff orders and licenses) as possible so that its commitment is viewed as genuine and irreversible by investors.[41] It is also been suggested that any new multi-year tariff system be included as a component of any proposed privatization agreement, as has been done in many other countries. However, it is unclear whether existing Indian regulatory commissions, which were set up to be "quasi-judicial" (like a court), could be parties to such a contract. If a commission cannot commit, can the government commit on its behalf once tariff-setting authority has been legally transferred to the regulatory commission?

Given this legal uncertainty, the better solution for India would probably be to amend the existing state electricity reform acts to mandate the use of multi-year tariffs—or, even better, to (1) transfer tariff-setting authority back to the government on a one-time basis for the initial post-privatization period, (2) incorporate the tariff-setting formula directly into the privatization agreement (which is the norm in almost every other country that has successfully privatized distribution) and (3) establish, via amendments to the existing state electricity laws, fairly detailed tariff principles and processes that would apply to subsequent multi-year tariff periods. Without such

---

40. For example, the Andhra Pradesh Electricity Regulatory Commission (2002) issued a consultative paper on long-term tariff-setting principles that, if adopted, would lead to a type of multi-year tariff. The paper is available at www.ercap.org/home.htm.

41. India is not the only country that may face a legal credibility problem. Turkey may encounter similar problems when it tries to privatize some of its government-owned distribution systems in the next year or two. Because the recently passed Turkish electricity law sets out only general tariff setting principles, any multi-year tariff system would have to be developed in secondary legislation. It remains to be seen as to whether investors will have confidence in the credibility of a tariff setting system that is limited to secondary legislation.

Box 2: The Delhi Privatizations: A Partial Regulatory Contract

"We never had any illusion that the whole world was dying to come and distribute power in Delhi."
—Jagdish Sagar, Chairman of DVB, *PowerLine*, June 2002

On July 1, 2002, the Delhi government sold a 51 percent equity interest in each of three new distribution companies that had been created out of DVB, the state-owned enterprise that had served the metropolitan area. At the time of privatization, DVB was a sick enterprise. It had technical and commercial losses of more than 50 percent and receivables of more US$400 million. Consumers were unhappy with the DVB's quality of service and the endemic corruption. For several years the Delhi government had been forced to prop up DVB with annual subsidies of US$200 to 300 million through loans that no one expected would be repaid. As one Indian official observed: "The government was hemorrhaging through the company and was getting absolutely nothing in return."

The negotiated sale to BSES and Tata Power, two private Indian companies, was the first major distribution privatization after several failed efforts elsewhere in India. It represents what could be the first example of a second generation of distribution privatizations in India. If successful, it will be an impressive accomplishment.*

The tariff system created for the Delhi privatization represents a *partial regulatory contract*. When it appeared that the government's efforts to privatize would fall victim to regulatory uncertainty, the Delhi government decided to issue a "policy directive" to the regulator. The directive obligated the regulator to (1) accept realistic initial values for technical and commercial losses, (2) adjust tariffs based on the loss improvement trajectory proposed by the bidders and accepted by the government, and (3) allow for the automatic pass-through of subsidized prices that the discos would pay for power purchased from the government-owned transco (transmission company).

The policy directive created a "partial" regulatory contract in that only some of the performance elements (i.e., loss improvements) and cost elements (i.e., bulk supply costs) were specified on a multi-year basis. Other elements, such as operating expenses and capital expenses, will continue to be reviewed and approved by the regulator on a year-to-year basis using general criteria rather than by specific formula. In contrast, the tariff-setting systems used in most Latin America (except for Brazil) are more completely specified. Other Indian states are now considering more-complete, multi-year tariff-setting systems that would be closer to the Latin American model. In at least one of these states, there has been discussion of implementing the new system by amending the existing state law to permit the state government to issue a one-time tariff directive for an initial, multi-year, post-privatization tariff period.

Apart from the incompleteness of the tariff regime, the regulatory contract was incomplete in one other important respect. The privatization went forward without an explicit *license* that spelled out the obligations and responsibilities of the new companies. The commission began developing such licenses only after privatization. The absence of a license prior to privatization obviously creates unnecessary uncertainty and disputes that could have been avoided.

---

* For a more complete description of the privatization by one of its principal proponents, see Sagar (2002).

changes, any privatization will take place under a cloud of legal uncertainty. (The Delhi government has adopted some elements of this strategy; see Box 2.)

Objections to Multi-year Tariffs

There are likely to be several objections to the multi–year tariff approach. The first is that it would compromise the independence of the existing Indian commissions. We think that this is a misplaced criticism. *The concept of independence does not logically require that a regulatory commission design the tariff system that it implements.* In many Latin American countries, independent regulatory commissions have been administering tariff-setting systems that were established by governments before the commissions came into existence.

A second objection is that it would put government back into the business of setting tariffs, which would undermine the principal rationale for creating independent regulatory commissions in the first place. But because the closing of the large revenue-cost gap that currently exists in most Indian states is inherently a political decision, it seems inevitable and necessary that the government must design and initiate the tariff-setting system for the first tariff-setting period and then provide detailed guidance on how it should be applied in later periods. Because the government has a strong incentive to get viable bids from private investors, it is more likely to "get it right" than an existing independent regulator operating under general tariff guidelines, which is the current norm throughout most of India.

The third objection is that the existing data are too unreliable to support a multi-year tariff system. It is argued that it is hard enough to set tariffs on a yearly basis, much less for several years. It is also claimed that a regulatory contract that embodies a multi-year tariff is not feasible in India until there are significant improvements in data quality.[42] The problem with this argument is that the data are not likely to get better under government ownership. Indian regulators have been demanding improvements in data from the state-owned utilities for several years with very little success.[43]

This argument also fails to recognize that significant gaps in data have been the norm rather than the exception in most distribution privatizations around the world. In a letter to the Andhra Pradesh regulatory commission, Professor Stephen Littlechild, the first electricity regulator in England and Wales, observed that "the Government [at the time of privatization] essentially said 'Let the companies have revenue equal to the present level increased by annual inflation plus a small annual amount X to reflect the need for higher capital expenditure'" with the expectation that the quality of data would improve (which it did) during the first multi-year tariff-setting period.[44]

A related concern in India is that private companies will be able to take advantage of the poor quality of data to earn high profits that would be a political embarrassment. Although this does not seem very likely given the large initial gap between costs and revenues, it could be addressed by including a profit or revenue-sharing mechanism as one element of the multi-year tariff system. The Delhi government recently adopted this approach by requiring a 50/50 split of all earned revenues above certain annual targeted technical and commercial loss-reduction levels. Although this is the functional equivalent of an extra income tax on the distribution companies, it does enhance the political acceptability of privatization.[45]

---

42. In a recent discussion of the new Indian electricity regulatory commissions (ERCs), it was noted that "All these ERCs have appreciated the need [adopting multi-year tariffs] for doing so but have expressed their inability in the matter, particularly due to the limitations and unreliability of data." See Godbole (2002).

43. In a recent tariff order, the electricity regulatory commission of the Indian state of Haryana observed that "in spite of this being the third filing of ARR [annual revenue requirement] by Haryana Vidyut Prasaran Nigam [state-owned electric utility], the information as required has not been furnished completely and therefore the commission had no option to grant a number of waivers which were granted last year also." Quoted in Godbole (2002).

44. Letter of Professor Stephen C. Littlechild to the Chairman and Members of the Andhra Pradesh Electricity Regulatory Commission, November 4, 2001.

45. For a negative appraisal of profit (as opposed to revenue) sharing, see Mayer and Vickers (1996).

CHAPTER 5

THE DETAILS OF THE REGULATORY CONTRACT: WHO BEARS WHAT RISK?

Overview of Risks

Many of the disagreements in designing a regulatory contract involve disagreements over whether the company, its customers or the government should bear a particular risk. Table 3 shows the key risks that exist for a new private distribution company and its lenders. From a potential investor's perspective, the allocation of risk in the regulatory contract will ultimately affect one of three things: the prices that it can charge, the costs that it can recover and the quantity of electricity that it can sell.

Investors and regulators look at risks from different perspectives. Investors ask: What risks am I being asked to bear? How much will it cost to bear this risk? Will I be compensated for bearing this risk? Governments and regulators ask different questions: Would it be fair for government or consumers to bear this risk? Who will get blamed if something goes wrong?

Not surprisingly, an almost universal rule of privatization is that *everyone wants someone else to bear the major risks*. It is generally agreed that the best principle for risk allocation is that a particular risk should be borne by the party that can mitigate or manage the risk at the lowest cost.[46] But although the principle is easy to state, there is often considerable disagreement over how it should be applied in particular situations. This can be seen in a more detailed analysis of four of the risks listed in Table 3: pass-through of power-purchase costs, loss-reduction targets, foreign exchange fluctuations, and obligation to supply.[47]

---

46. This principle is often misinterpreted. For example, a distribution company may be given the responsibility for mitigating a particular risk (e.g., the risk of future price fluctuations in purchased power) because the distribution company can mitigate the risk at lower cost than anyone else. But the costs incurred by the distribution company to bear this risk will almost always be paid for by its customers.

47. The general form (such as a price cap, revenue cap, or a combination of the two) will have a significant effect on the allocation of risk between the company and its consumers. For an excellent discussion of this issue, see Alexander and Shugart (1999).

TABLE 3: MAJOR RISKS FOR DISTRIBUTION COMPANIES AND THEIR LENDERS

Risk	Explanation
Collection Risk	Risk that the company will be unable to collect its allowed revenues. This might occur for one or more of the following reasons: customers refuse to pay their bills, customers tamper or disconnect meters, company employees receive bribes to make illegal connections or under collect metered or billed amounts, and government officials or courts are unable or unwilling to support disconnections or other actions against non-paying customers.
Power-purchase Risk	Risk that the company will not be allowed to charge tariffs that recover the cost of its power purchases. This could occur if the regulator disallows the prices paid or the quantities purchased.
Demand Risk	Risk that the quantity of electricity sold is less than the amount projected by the company or the regulator in setting tariffs.
Obligation-to-Supply Risk	Risk that the company will collect lower revenues and/or pay penalties because it is unable to meet supply obligations specified in its license or concession. The company's failure to supply may be caused by its own actions (e.g., poor transformer maintenance), actions of others (e.g., inadequate generation or transmission capacity) or acts of God (e.g., a major drought).
Operating Cost Risk	Risk that the company will not be able to recover the costs of operating its distribution system (i.e., the "wires" function) or the costs of retailing electricity (i.e., the supply function) either because the regulator disallows certain operating costs or sets unrealistic performance targets. The allowance for some technical and non-technical losses is sometimes included as operating costs.
Capital Cost Risk	Risk that the company will not be able to recover its capital costs because the regulator sets a low allowed capital base, disallows costs of certain capital expenditures, or sets low rates of return.
Inflation Risk	Risk that company's tariff will not be adjusted for general inflation.
Foreign Exchange Rate Risk	Risk that the company will not receive sufficient revenues from its customers to pay for costs incurred in "hard" currencies.
Foreign Exchange Convertibility Risk	Risk that the government will not give the company access to sufficient foreign exchange to repatriate earnings and to pay for costs incurred in other currencies.
Financing Risk	Risks related to the financial risks borne by entities that have lent money to the company.
Regulatory Risk	Risk that the regulator will reinterpret existing regulations or create new ones that will increase costs or reduce revenues.
Political Risk	Risks of expropriation, nationalization, war, civil disturbances and breach of contracts.
Government Subsidy Risk	Risk that the government does not pay promised subsidies or pays with considerable delay.

Passing-Through the Cost of Power Purchases

The biggest risk for any new private distribution company is that it will not be allowed to recover the costs of its power purchases for captive customers. Partial or delayed pass-through of power-purchase costs could bankrupt a distribution company because these costs usually constitute about 50 to 80 percent of its total costs.[48] Therefore, it is not surprising that most private investors seek total and automatic pass-through of all power-purchase costs, notwithstanding high power prices[49] and sometimes diverging definitions of the term *automatic* (see Box 3). They argue that such costs are largely beyond their control.

In contrast, regulators are generally fearful and suspicious of automatic pass-through mechanisms. Their concern is that automatic pass-through will lead to inefficient and sloppy buying practices, "sweetheart deals" (i.e., paying above-market prices for purchases from affiliated generators or marketers) or even intentional overpayments to generators from distributors in return for a hidden "kickback." Most regulators believe that the purchases will not be "economical" unless the company bears some risk of non-recovery through a benchmark or some other regulatory mechanism.[50]

Regulation of power purchases does not exist in isolation. Any regulatory mechanism designed to encourage economical purchasing will inevitably affect the incentives to build new generating capacity. Consider the case of a regulator that sets a low ceiling on the price of power purchases that a distribution company can pass through to its retail customers. Although the cap may be formally applied just to the distributor, it is, in effect, also a cap on generators because no rational distributor will sign a contract to buy electricity from generators at prices higher than the prices that it is allowed to recover from its retail customers. However, the distributor cannot stop buying if it has an obligation to serve. So even if it no longer purchases power under contracts, it will still have to buy in a spot or balancing market that may have even higher prices.

The regulator is then faced with the decision of whether to allow the spot or balancing market prices to be passed through to retail customers. If it allows pass-through, consumers will end up paying the higher prices that the regulator was trying to block, the only difference is that the higher prices will come through spot rather than contract purchases. If the regulator refuses to allow pass-through of the higher spot prices, then it may bankrupt the distribution company (which happened in California). If the regulator imposes a power-purchase ceiling price on both spot and contract purchases, generators may refuse to generate electricity—if not openly, then indirectly by finding an unexpected need to perform lengthy maintenance on their generating units.

---

48. This is exactly what happened in California. In the fall of 2000, PG & E and Southern California Edison, the two largest distribution companies, were buying power that averaged 20 cents per kilowatt-hour and were required to resell that power to their retail customers at about 6 cents per kilowatt-hour. By the time the California regulatory commission decided to raise the average retail rate, it was too late—PG & E was already in bankruptcy and Southern California Edison was teetering on the brink. See Besant-Jones and Tenenbaum (2001).

49. A guaranteed automatic pass through is of little comfort to a distribution company if it is being forced to accept high-priced power. Even though the distribution company may have been granted a clear legal right to pass through the power-purchase costs, it may be politically or economically impossible to exercise this legal right if the price is too high. Such a concern was recently raised by the only bidder for the Uganda distribution system and was also one of the reasons given by AES when it withdrew from Orissa in India. To deal with this concern, the government of Delhi guaranteed a five-year, subsidized price for power supplied to any winning bidder in the recent privatization of the Delhi distribution systems.

50. In theory, the need for a regulator to review power purchase costs arises only when a distribution company has captive customers. It has sometimes been assumed that there is no need for a regulator to review the reasonableness of power purchase costs when there is full retail competition (i.e., all retail customers have the right to choose their supplier). But even with full retail competition, many small consumers will choose to remain customers of their existing distribution companies because it is simply not worth the time to sort through competing offers for the amount of money that is likely to be saved. Other customers with poor payment records may find that no supplier wants to supply them because they are deemed to be too risky. In both situations, regulators will find themselves under pressure to protect these customers from inefficient or dishonest purchases by the local distribution company. For a good discussion of these issues, see Hunt (2002).

Box 3: AUTOMATIC PASS-THROUGH: IT'S NOT WHAT YOU SAY, IT'S WHAT YOU DO

Some Brazilian officials describe their power-purchase pass-through mechanism as an example of "full" or "automatic" pass-through. This normally means that the regulatory contract provides for frequent and complete adjustments for changes in power-purchases costs. But in fact, this has not been the case because Brazilian law allows the Brazilian electricity regulator to make adjustments in retail tariffs *only once a year*. The general prohibition on more frequent adjustments reflects a macroeconomic concern that indexing or any regulatory mechanism that mimics indexing (e.g., automatic monthly tariff adjustments to reflect changes in power-purchase costs) could lead to a new outbreak of the hyperinflation that Brazil experienced during the 1990s.

This economy-wide, legal prohibition on more-frequent price adjustments has created significant financial risk for Brazilian distribution companies. For example, suppose that a distribution company's retail tariff were set on the assumption that its dollar-denominated power-purchase costs will be US$1 million dollars (3 million reales in Brazilian currency) per month. If the real declines in value against the dollar by 10 percent, the distribution company will need to pay 300,000 more reales per month to its power supplier. Because Brazilian law prohibits it from adjusting its retail tariffs until the next scheduled annual tariff adjustment, it will be losing 300,000 reales per month. And when retail rates are finally changed the following year to reflect the higher power-purchase costs, there is no "catch-up" mechanism to recover the money that the company lost in every month since the previous adjustment.

In fact, this was the situation in Brazil until October 2001. Brazilian distribution companies paid for a significant share of their power purchases (e.g., imported power and power from the bi-national Itaipu dam) in dollars and were allowed to recover these costs in Brazilian reales in tariffs that could be adjusted only once a year. ElectroPaulo, one of the distribution utilities serving Sao Paulo, has estimated that it lost about US$180 million between June 1999 and October 2001 because its automatic pass-through mechanism permitted only annual adjustments for cost changes.

There are two principal solutions to the mismatch between cost changes and tariff adjustments. The first is to allow for more frequent adjustments. This is the system that exists in Bolivia (monthly), most of the United States (monthly) and the Indian state of Haryana (quarterly). The second is to create a *tracking account*, the approach adopted by the Brazilian regulator in October 2001. This involves depositing the differences (both positive and negative) between projected and actual power-purchase costs into a special internal account. At the time of the next annual adjustment, the amount of money in the tracking account is added to or subtracted from the then-current level of power-purchase costs. If the distribution company is also allowed to earn interest on the money that accumulates in the tracking account, it is made financially "whole" (that is, it does not lose money on the lag in tariff adjustment). In the case of Brazil, the tracking account is "emptied" once a year and consequently does not violate the legal prohibition on more frequent adjustments.

Tracking accounts do, however, have problems. They can lead to big tariff increases at the time of the next adjustment, and a distribution company could experience a significant cash shortfall until the adjustment is actually made. Nicaragua has tried to deal with the first problem by creating a pre-specified "trigger" that empties the account if the account balance would produce a tariff increase above a specified size.

So although regulators may have had the best of intentions in imposing a cap (i.e., protecting consumers from inefficient purchases), consumers will ultimately be hurt if investors are unwilling to finance new generating plants—which, in turn, may lead to rationing and blackouts. In imposing such caps, there is a tendency for new regulators to think of themselves as "masters of the universe" and to not think through the likely effects of their actions. As one Eastern European regulator has observed, regulators forget (or perhaps never realize) that "it is impossible to cheat economics: every investment must be feasible."[51]

---

51. Attributed to the Chairman of the Polish electricity commission in *Power in East Europe*, June 2, 2000, p. 10.

Purchases Where the Distributor Does Not Have Discretion

In designing a regulatory contract, the easiest cases involve purchases through "vesting contracts" or from "single buyers." The former refers to power-purchase contracts that are assigned to distribution companies at the time of privatization. Typically, such contracts oblige the distribution company to buy a certain quantity of electricity from one or more generators at specified price for a certain number of years. Because such contracts are usually assigned to distributors by the government as part of the privatization package, a new distribution company is not able to affect the terms and conditions of the contracts (see Box 4).

Therefore, it is reasonable for the privatization agreement to require the current or future regulator to allow automatic pass-through of all vesting contract costs.[52] Similarly, if there is a

---

BOX 4: WHAT COSTS CAN THE DISTRIBUTOR CONTROL?

The heart of any regulatory contract is the tariff-setting system. Most regulatory contracts specify a multi-year system that includes a formula that distinguishes between controllable and non-controllable costs. The distinction is usually based on an assessment of a disco's ability to influence a particular cost.* Changes in non-controllable costs are automatically passed through to retail customers in the tariff-setting formula. In contrast, changes in controllable costs are not automatically passed through. Instead, they are benchmarked and the disco may earn a reward or penalty depending on its performance relative to the benchmark. A variety of benchmarks exist, the most common being the performance of other distribution companies (discos), an external index or the company's own past performance. (Appendix A describes a regulatory framework proposed in a South Asian country for dealing with controllable and non-controllable costs.)

A common mistake made in designing a multi-year tariff system is that the government or the regulator will fail to distinguish between degrees of effective control. For a particular input, a disco may have control over the input price, the input quantity, or both. For example, if a disco is assigned a vesting contract at the time of privatization or is required to purchase from a single specified seller, it will have no control over the price of power purchased. But even if it cannot influence price, it will still have control over the quantity purchased because the latter will depend on its ability to reduce technical and commercial losses. In this case, then, it is appropriate to allow automatic pass-through of the price of power, while benchmarking the quantity. For later post-privatization bulk-power purchases, the disco may have control over price and quantity, and both should be benchmarked.

The nature of control over a particular cost item may be quite different between developed and developing countries. For example, in developed countries that have introduced bulk power competition, the price that a disco pays for power may depend greatly on its purchasing skills. Even if the bulk power market is highly competitive, this in itself is no guarantee that the disco will be an effective buyer. Therefore, the price of power purchases is often benchmarked to try to encourage better performance. In contrast, the quantity of power purchased is usually a pass-through because the disco is likely to have achieved close-to-optimal technical efficiency and commercial losses will be very small.

In most developing countries the situation is quite different. When a private company takes over from a state-owned enterprise, it is not uncommon for the private company to start operations with loss levels of 30 to 60 percent, largely due to theft and corruption. The biggest potential for cost reductions will be in the quantity of power that the discos purchase and not necessarily in its price. Therefore, it makes sense in most developing countries to focus on setting targets for commercial and technical losses (which indirectly establish a target for the quantity of electricity purchased) because the inefficiencies are large and the opportunities for improvement are significant.

---

* A good discussion of controllable and non-controllable costs for Indian distribution companies can be found in Alexander and Harris (2001).

---

52. Such a policy has been implemented or proposed in the distribution concession and license agreements in Argentina, Moldova, Georgia and Brazil.

single buyer who has a legal monopoly to buy on behalf of all distributors, the prices of the single buyer's purchases (which may have been inherited by the single buyer or previously reviewed by the regulator) will generally be automatically passed through in the retail tariffs of distributors.[53]

In both cases, there is little or no risk to investors unless the pass-through is delayed or incomplete. But there is a risk of public pressure to renege on the contracts if the vesting contract uses a formula that fixes prices at a significantly higher level than observed spot-market prices.

Purchases Where the Distributor Has Discretion

The more difficult case involves new, post-privatization power purchases in which the distribution entity has some discretion over the purchases made and the prices paid. The regulatory treatment of such purchases will vary depending on whether or not there is an organized bulk power market.

Where an Organized Market Exists

In situations where there is organized market, the natural inclination of the regulator or the government is to write a regulatory contract that uses the market price, either estimated or actual, as a benchmark against which to judge the prices paid by the distributors. Although it seems reasonable to use a market benchmark, this can have unintended consequences.

Ex ante *spot-market benchmarks.* In Argentina, distribution companies regulated by ENRE (the national electricity regulator) are allowed to pass through an estimate of future, geographically differentiated spot prices that are referred to as "seasonal nodal prices." These estimates are made by the system operator (CAMMESA) based on estimates of what the nodal prices will be six months into the future and are recalculated every six months. One unexpected consequence of this regulatory policy is that distribution companies have little or no incentive to enter into long-term contracts because they have the "no risk" option of automatically passing through the estimated nodal prices to consumers. In such a situation, a long-term contract is a risky option for a distribution company because the price in the long-term contract could turn out to be higher than the nodal prices allowed by the regulator. As a consequence, this well-intentioned regulatory policy appears to have caused a dramatic decline in the proportion of purchases made under long-term contracts by private Argentine distribution companies.[54] It has been estimated that long-term purchases constituted about 60 percent of distribution company power purchases at the beginning of the reforms in 1992. By 2000, the average percentage had dropped to about 20 percent.

The problems are often exacerbated if the regulator or some other government or quasi-governmental body is responsible for calculating the spot market benchmark. For example, in Peru the benchmark for the estimated future price of power purchases is calculated by COES, the system operator whose decisions appear to be strongly influenced by the government power enterprises represented on its board. It is relatively easy to manipulate the estimates because they are based on projections of average expected spot prices four years into the future in contrast to the three-month projections in Argentina. Since 1997, COES has calculated the allowed power-purchase pass-through price for distribution companies based on its prediction that there would be significant new gas-fired generation because of the completion of a new gas pipeline from the

---

53. This has been the approach in countries or regions such as Poland, Hungary and Orissa (India) that have relied on the single buyer model. Until the early 1990s, it was also the norm in many parts of the United States where privately-owned vertically integrated utilities were the sole suppliers for captive municipal and cooperative distribution systems that were known as "full requirements customers."

54. In June 2001, the Argentine government proposed a major change in the power-purchase pass-through mechanism. It proposed that distributors be required to purchase a large percentage of their new supplies of electricity through competitive bidding (under guidelines specified by the regulator). The government proposed replacing the estimated nodal price ceilings with automatic pass through of the actual winning bids. This proposal of mandatory competitive bidding, which was one part of larger power sector reform package, was rejected by the Argentine congress. If adopted, it would have been similar to a system that currently exists in Panama.

Camisea basin to metropolitan Lima. This prediction had the effect of lowering the ceiling price for purchased power and the prices charged to retail customers. Although these low retail prices allowed the government to claim success for the power reform program, it conflicted with the reality that the pipeline was not completed by early 2003. Within the Peruvian power sector, these non-existent gas fired plants came to be referred to as the "ghosts of Camisea." But these ghost plants, by lowering the allowed pass-through price for power purchases, had the real-world consequence of discouraging further private investment in new generating plants.[55]

There are three basic problems with creating benchmarks that rely exclusively on spot or nodal prices. The first problem, as noted above, is that it creates a strong incentive for distributors to buy in just the spot market. This, in turn, creates disincentives for new investment in generation. Most generators will not be willing to take the risk of building new plants on the basis of frequently revised estimates of spot or nodal prices, particularly if the benchmark prices are calculated by the regulator or a government-controlled entity, which is the prevailing situation in several Latin American countries (Argentina, Bolivia, Chile, El Salvador, and Peru).[56] These disincentives have been counterbalanced to some degree by the facts that (1) the generators are also eligible to receive a "generation capacity payment" that can provide a second and more stable source of revenues and (2) the capacity payments are automatically passed through to retail customers.

A second problem is that it forces consumers to bear the risk of future price fluctuations in the spot market unless the benchmark is based on multi-year estimates of spot market prices (as in Chile and Peru). Although consumers may actually prefer that the distribution company engage in hedging activities on their behalf, there is no regulatory incentive for the company to do so.[57]

The third and more fundamental problem is that it reflects a naïve view of bulk power markets—one that fails to recognize that bulk power can be purchased under a variety of terms and conditions. Any regulatory pass-through mechanism that presumes that spot prices are the only "true prices" will distort the behavior of distributors and generators and lead to bad outcomes.

Ideally, a regulatory contract should a give a distribution company the incentive to acquire a portfolio of purchases—some long, some short, some firm, some non-firm. But such a system will work only if the regulator is willing to accept that a distribution company must function as more than a passive entity that simply passes through spot or nodal prices to its captive customers. The simple truth is that no distributor will be a motivated buyer unless it is allowed to recover its hedging costs and has a reasonable possibility to earn profits on its purchasing activities.

Ex ante *or* ex post *multi-market price caps.*   In 1999, OFFER, the British regulator, established a supply cap (that is, a cap on power-purchase costs) for 12 distribution companies that contained an 11 percent premium above its estimate of future spot market prices to encourage hedging. It was left up to the distribution companies to decide how they would hedge. Although the benchmark was based on estimated spot market prices, the 11 percent premium created an explicit incentive for British distribution companies to try to beat the spot market prices by signing longer-term contracts at pre-specified prices or using other hedging instruments.[58]

---

55. More recently, the Peruvian spokesman for Duke Energy was attributed as saying that the November 2001 calculation of benchmark nodal prices included a hydro plant that was not in service. See "Duke Pulls Out of Egasa and Egusur Sales," *Reuters News Service*, May 9, 2002.

56. Peru, Chile and Bolivia have tried to overcome this disincentive by imposing an additional requirement on distribution companies that they buy a high percentage of their supply needs under long-term contracts. Bolivia requires that its distribution companies buy 80 percent of their supply needs in contracts that have a duration of at least three years. Chile and Peru require that their distribution companies obtain 100 percent of their supply needs in contracts that are one year or longer. But this regulatory requirement is unenforceable if distributors are unable to find generators are willing to sell to them at prices that will change every three months based on estimates made by a regulator or system operator who is under political pressure to keep the estimates low.

57. For a discussion of the theory and practice of hedging of purchases by electric and gas distribution companies, see Fernando and Kleindoerfer (1997) and Costello (2002).

58. OFGEM (1999).

Similar incentives also existed through an explicit, *ex post* multi-market benchmark created by the Dutch regulator. In the Netherlands, 50 percent of a distribution company's allowed power-purchase costs were based, until recently, on a benchmark keyed to the average cost of power purchases by all distribution companies over a three-month period.[59] The average cost was based on all purchases, not just spot market purchases.

The Dutch mechanism resembles a similar mechanism that was created by the Colombian regulator in 1997. Distribution companies in Colombia are allowed to automatically pass through about 80 to 90 percent of their power-purchase costs. However, pass-through of the remaining 10 to 20 percent is keyed to a benchmark rather than to actual power-purchase costs. The benchmark is based on average prices paid by all distribution companies for all purchases (i.e., spot, intermediate and long-term purchases). Even though Colombia, unlike other Latin American countries, has no requirement that a distribution company acquire any specified portion of its supplies from long-term contracts, the *ex post*, all-market benchmark has created a strong incentive for distribution companies to pursue a mix of purchases. In 2000, Colombian distribution companies purchased about 10 to 20 percent of their supplies in the spot market. The remaining supplies were purchased under a variety of contract forms and durations. If a Colombian distributor "beats" the benchmark, it can keep the savings as additional profits.

The *ex post, multi-market* benchmarks of the Netherlands and Colombia have several advantages:

- The regulator does not need to pre-specify an optimal pattern of spot and contract purchases.
- The regulator does not need to conduct after-the-fact "prudence" reviews of the distribution company's purchasing practices.
- It creates an incentive for distributors to engage in hedging practices.
- It creates a disincentive for distributors to pay above-market prices to affiliated generators and marketers because they run the risk that they will not be able to pass on the inflated costs to their captive consumers.

Benchmarks are not perfect regulatory instruments, however. They will not be fair to any company that is always on the "wrong side of the benchmark" for reasons beyond its control.[60] Also, they are only feasible in countries where there are multiple distribution companies.

Where No Organized or Functioning Market Exists
Where there is no organized market or the market does not function, other approaches have to be established for determining the reasonableness of the distributor's discretionary purchases. These include the following:

- *Ex ante* administratively set price caps.
- Mandated competitive procurement under regulatory guidelines.
- *Ex ante* "reasonableness" reviews of PPAs.
- *Ex post* "reasonableness" reviews of PPAs.

Ex ante *administratively set price caps.*   As mentioned in Chapter 4, in Brazil the concession agreements for private distribution companies set the allowed pass-through of power-purchase costs to *valores normativos* (VNs). The VNs are ceiling prices that are administratively established

---

59. DTE (2002).

60. For example, a distribution company may always be above the benchmark if its customer mix is more costly to serve (e.g., it serves customers that in the aggregate produce a more peaked load curve). Or it may always have to pay a higher purchase price if it considered less creditworthy by generators (e.g., distribution companies serving an area with guerilla activity). For general discussion of some of the problems in the use of benchmarks by regulators, see Shuttleworth (1999).

by ANEEL, Brazil's national electricity regulator. Until recently, ANEEL opted to establish six separate price caps for different fuels and technology based on ANEEL's estimates of the long-term marginal cost of supplying electricity from that particular technology. Each approved power purchase is assigned a VN value at the time of approval by ANEEL, and this initial value is then partially indexed over the life of the purchase.

ANEEL's VN approach has been criticized for two reasons. First, generators have argued that the cap for thermal generation was too low, did not differentiate between peak and base load units, and did not adequately adjust for foreign exchange risk. The latter is especially important because thermal generators are forced to pay for their fuel (usually natural gas) in dollars but receive payments in reales (the Brazilian currency) for the electricity that they supply to distributors.

Second, the details of the formula were initially unclear. When the distributors were granted their concessions, the concessions indicated that pass-through of cost of power purchases in the "free market" (i.e., discretionary purchases) would be based on the VNs that would be determined by ANEEL, but there were few details as to how the VNs would actually be set. Since the inception of the VN system in August 1998, ANEEL has found it necessary to issue four additional regulations to modify or clarify the operation of the system. This suggests that the Brazilian "regulatory contract" was effectively a "non-contract" because the provisions covering the regulatory treatment of 50 to 60 percent of a distributor's costs were very general with the specifics were to be filled in later.

Mandated competitive procurement under regulatory guidelines.   Panama, Nicaragua, Guatemala have opted for a different approach, focusing on process rather than on outcomes. In these countries, the regulators have issued procurement guidelines that require distribution companies to acquire new supplies through competitive procurements.[61] Under the Panamanian regulations, a distribution company is allowed to pass through the costs of new purchases if it has followed the regulator's purchasing guidelines. Distributors in Panama have complained that they cannot get good prices because the regulator has over-specified the purchasing guidelines and is therefore acting more as a manager than a regulator.

In the United States, the New Jersey regulator, like its Panamanian counterpart, has also mandated competitive procurement by all distribution companies. New Jersey has full retail competition so every customer has the legal right to choose an alternate supplier. But the reality is that very few retail customers have exercised this right. So the procurement is essentially a procurement by the distribution companies to acquire the supplies needed to serve a pre-specified portion of the load of the customers who did not exercise their right to choose, or were not

---

61. For the Panamanian regulations, see www.enteregulador.gob.pa/electric/default.asp. A similar approach was proposed by the U.S. Federal Energy Regulatory Commission (FERC) in the late 1980s. The FERC issued a proposed competitive bidding rule and stated that if a utility followed these guidelines it would pre-commit to finding the purchase to be "just and reasonable." However, the rule was never issued in final form because, among other things, the state electricity regulatory commissions, which had jurisdiction over the retail tariffs of the buying utilities, complained that FERC did not have the authority to issue such guidelines. But on their own initiative several state commissions issued competitive procurement guidelines similar to the FERC guidelines for the utilities in their states. The U.S. power procurements in the late 80s and early 90s were always for physical contracts (i.e., contracts that gave the buying utility the right to make dispatch decisions) as opposed to the financial contracts (i.e, the seller commits to supply a specified amount of electricity at a specified price without ceding physical control over its supply source to the buyer) that currently exist in Central America. The use of procurements for physical contracts probably reflected the fact that the buyer was a vertically integrated utility who would integrate the purchase into its own portfolio of supply sources and who did not have access to well-functioning spot market. The guidelines issued by the U.S. state regulators usually required selection based on an assessment of both price and non-price factors. In contrast, in a typical procurement for a financial contract, the selection is almost always limited just to price. For a description of the U.S. experience with mandated competitive bidding, see Plummer and Troppman (1990).

given an offer by, an alternative supplier. The first auction, conducted by an independent third party, was completed in April 2001 and produced prices ranging from 4.86 to 5.81 cents per kwh. However, because the New Jersey distribution companies are also subject to a retail price cap, they could not automatically pass through the results of the mandatory procurement to their customers. If their overall costs (distribution costs plus power purchases) go above the statutory retail price cap, the "extra" costs are deferred (i.e., put into a tracking account) for possible recovery sometime in the future. So the New Jersey system is really a combination of three regulatory tools: mandatory competitive procurement for one year's worth of supplies, a mandatory retail price cap, and an after-the-fact review of the "prudence" of all costs (including power-purchase costs) that exceed the price cap.

Ex ante *"reasonableness" reviews of PPAs.*   A third approach is for the regulator to make before-the-fact reviews of proposed power-purchase agreements (PPAs) between generators and distributors before they go to financial closure. For example, the Andhra Pradesh regulatory commission in India recently questioned a number of provisions in a proposed PPA between a private generator and the state-owned utility (Andhra Pradesh Electricity Regulatory Commission, 2002b). As a general rule, this is an undesirable approach to reviewing power-purchase costs because (1) it introduces considerable uncertainty and slows down the procurement process, and (2) the considerable discretion it gives to the regulator may create enormous temptation for sellers to try to bribe the regulator to get the PPA approved, especially in those countries with a history of corruption.

Nevertheless, this may be the only option available to a regulator if it has jurisdiction over a state-owned utility that has been pressured into making uneconomic purchases negotiated by politicians and then handed over to the utility as a *fait accompli*. If the regulator simply accepts the PPAs, it will saddle the existing state-owned company or future private distribution companies with impossibly high power-purchase costs.[62] Acceptance by the regulator of uneconomic PPAs can be a major impediment to any future attempts to privatize distribution.

Ex post *"reasonableness" reviews of PPAs.*   Regulators may conduct a "prudence" or "reasonableness" review after a PPA has been signed and gone to financial closure. This is the worst kind of regulatory review because it creates an enormous amount of uncertainty. If it becomes the dominant regulatory mode, most investors will consider the country to be a risky place to do business and will demand a risk premium that will ultimately be paid for by consumer. But, once again, it may be the only plausible option for a regulator that is seriously trying to protect consumer interests if it suspects that a state-owned utility was pressured into signing a PPA by corrupt government officials who may have received bribes from the generator. The trade-off for the regulator is between protecting consumers from paying prices that may reflect corruption versus increasing the perception that the country is risky for infrastructure projects. Unfortunately, such reviews are often conducted by officials of a subsequent government or politicians from another political party rather than the regulator.[63] When this happens, there is always a suspicion that the review may be motivated more by a desire to discredit one's political opponents than a genuine interest in protecting consumer interests. Therefore, such reviews, whether conducted by the regulator or other government officials, should be used as a "last resort" only when there is persuasive evidence of outright corruption.

After-the-fact "reasonableness" reviews have been a routine regulatory tool even in developed countries. For example, in the early 1990s the California energy regulator routinely conducted *ex post*

---

62. This seems to have happened in Pakistan, Guatemala, the Dominican Republic and the Philippines.

63. As this is being written, there is a major controversy in the Philippines over a number of IPPs contracts signed by the state-owned utility. A Philippine politician recently called for a Senate inquiry that "should probe deep into the technical and financial specifications of the expensive contracts." See *Manila Bulletin*, "Five Costliest IPP-Napocor Contracts Listed," August 19, 2002.

procurement reviews to assess the "reasonableness" of purchases made by gas distribution utilities serving that state. In the words of one gas company official, these reviews were "time consuming and frustrating, and left everyone angry because no one got what they wanted."[64] A long-time California consumer advocate similarly described the "retrospective reasonableness reviews" as counterproductive and ultimately harmful to consumers because they created strong incentives for the distribution company to make purchases "to avoid regulatory disallowance rather than trying to minimize costs."[65] In general, *ex post* reviews have several major weaknesses: they tend to focus only on extreme examples of incompetence or inefficiency, they provide no penalties for failure to adopt best practices, they offer no rewards for superior performance, and they tend to drag on and on.[66]

Perhaps realizing that this was a costly and invasive form of regulation that generally did not benefit anyone other than lawyers and expert witnesses, the California commission replaced its *ex post* review system with an *ex ante* price benchmark system in the late 1990s. Under the new benchmarking system, utilities were given the opportunity to earn profits if they were able to purchase gas at average prices lower than the benchmark prices. The consumer advocate described the new benchmark system as a superior regulatory approach because it "created a partnership between shareholders and ratepayers by aligning their interests."

Loss-Reduction Targets

Power purchases raise two questions for a regulatory contract. The first issue, discussed in the previous chapter, involves the *prices* that the regulator will allow for such purchases. The second issue is the *quantity* of power purchases that the regulator will allow the disco to recover in tariffs. This second determination depends largely on the *level of losses* on the disco system that is deemed to be acceptable. Losses can be thought of as "whatever happens in the great unknown middle" between the quantity of electricity received at the transmission-distribution interface and the quantity of money received by the distribution company for electricity that is metered, billed and collected from its customers. In India, recent estimates of overall losses for some of the existing state-owned distribution systems are as high as 50 percent.[67] This means that for every two kilowatt-hours purchased, the distribution company is able to collect money from customers for only one.[68] The other kilowatt-hour somehow just "disappears."

Types of Losses

The overall losses on a distribution system comprise both technical and a non-technical losses. Technical losses are the engineering losses that arise because of the design and physical operation of the distribution grid. For example, a distribution system with longer feeders will usually show

---

64. See Gee (2001).

65. Procta (2001).

66. In the case of one California gas distribution utility, the final regulatory decision on the utility's 1994 purchases was not made until 2000.

67. In India, the reported numbers have gone up over the last several years. It is probably not because losses have actually increased but because reporting has become more truthful as governments try to get the state-owned companies ready for privatization. There is widespread anecdotal evidence that state-owned power companies routinely hid their actual losses in overestimates of consumption by agricultural customers. This is relatively easy to do because most agricultural consumption has generally not been metered in India since the 1980s. A recent study of the irrigation pumpset consumption in the state of Haryana found that farmers were actually consuming 27 percent less electricity than the state-owned utility attributed to them. If this result, based on a sample of 584 pumpsets, is extrapolated to the entire state, it would imply that Haryana's actual transmission and distribution losses would be 47 percent rather than the officially reported 33 percent. See Monari (2002).

68. For example, if a distribution company pays US$1 for a unit of electricity and then loses half of its purchased units and then only collects on 70 percent of what it bills, it will end up receiving revenues of US$.35 for each US$1.00 of power purchase costs.

higher losses because more electricity is lost with increases in the distance that the electricity has to be transported. Non-technical losses are commercial losses that result from theft (sometimes with the active assistance of distribution company employees), absence of metering, inaccurate metering, under-billing and poor collections. These commercial losses are referred to in Latin America as "black losses." The level of commercial losses very much depends on managerial efforts. In many developing countries, commercial losses will often be two to three times larger than technical losses. Reductions in technical losses reduce the cost of power purchases while reductions in commercial losses increase revenues. The inability of state-owned power systems in Central Asia, South Asia, Central America and Africa to achieve financial viability is largely attributable to commercial losses.

In dealing with losses, the two key design questions in a regulatory contract are: What should be the initial accepted level of overall losses for tariff-setting purposes? And: How quickly can losses be reduced? The answers to these two questions determine how the cost of losses is allocated between the company and its customers. In some countries of Latin America, technical and non-technical losses were estimated to be as high as 30 to 40 percent prior to privatization. Most private distribution companies in Latin America have had considerable success in reducing losses. In Chile, overall losses were reduced by more than 50 percent in seven years. In Argentina, similar reductions were achieved in even less time.[69] (See Box 5 for a discussion of implementation issues in setting loss reduction targets.)

Reducing losses can lead to significantly higher profits. For example, in one medium-sized Latin American distribution company of about 400,000 customers, it was estimated that a 1 percent reduction in commercial losses added about US$400,000 to the company's net revenues. As some private Latin American distribution companies now move into their second post-privatization tariff-setting periods, they are approaching overall loss levels that are close to the 8 to 10 percent levels observed in some Western European countries. This is an enormous change from where the loss levels were 10 years ago.

Can Latin America's Success be Repeated in Africa and India?

It is tempting to predict that such improvements can be repeated in India or Africa or elsewhere. But this overlooks two important features of the Latin American privatizations that may not exist in India or Africa. First, in Latin America the new private owners generally were given full control over their labor force at the time of privatization or shortly thereafter. Consequently, they retained only the people they wanted. In contrast, most of the proposed privatizations in India require the new owners keep existing employees under the previous terms and conditions of their employment contract for several years. Therefore, new private companies in India will probably be less successful in reducing losses because some of their employees will be able to sabotage any efforts that force them to give up money currently earned by promoting theft by customers. (In some parts of India, this form of theft is euphemistically referred to as "the micro-privatization problem.")[70]

---

69. The Argentinian and Chilean governments included technical loss-reduction targets in the concession agreements for newly privatized distribution companies. In contrast, the Brazilian government established no loss-reduction targets for newly privatized distribution companies. This means that the distribution companies have been allowed to pass through the full quantity of power purchased. In its February 2003 proposals for the second, multi-year tariff period of two distribution companies, the Brazilian regulator has stated that it now intends to establish loss-reduction targets rather than just accepting the full quantity of power purchases.

70. In a random sample of Indian electricity consumers, about 30 percent reported paying bribes to employees of power enterprises. Usually, the bribes were paid to linesmen, meter readers and billing employees. This is probably an underestimate for two reasons. First, the survey was limited to individuals and therefore does not capture bribes paid by corporations. Second, it probably fails to capture consumer initiated corruption. See Transparency International (2002).

Box 5: Adjusting for Losses: Specific Implementation Issues

In the tariff-setting formula, the adjustment for losses is usually done through a "grossing up" mechanism. For example, if a distribution utility meters and bills 100 units of electricity from its customers, the regulator in a developed country would normally allow the company to charge its customers the cost of purchasing 108 to 112 units of electricity from the disco's bulk suppliers. However, in a developing country where theft has been rampant, the regulator (or the regulatory contract negotiated by the government prior to privatization) may include a formula that assumes that the company will have to buy 140 to 150 units of electricity for every 100 units that it bills its customers.

"Grossing up" can be used to account for both technical and commercial losses. For technical losses, the gross-up adjustment allows for the recovery of the cost of electricity that is physically lost on the distribution system. Technical losses depend on both the design and operation of the system. For commercial losses, the gross-up allows discos to recover the cost of power that is stolen. The gross up for commercial losses allows the discos to charge paying customers for electricity stolen by non-paying customers.

In most developing countries where meters do not exist or have been tampered with, there are always disputes over the initial assumed level of losses (the "initializing value") and the required rate of improvement (the "loss-reduction trajectory"). In India, for example, there is widespread anecdotal evidence that the state-owned enterprises systematically underestimated their losses by claiming that their unmetered agricultural customers were consuming more electricity than they actually were. Over the last several years, as many state-owned utilities are being prepared for privatization, these utilities have made substantial upward revisions in their overall loss estimates. (In Orissa, the number was raised from 19 percent to 42.6 percent.)

The grossing up can be performed on different bases relating to retail consumption: metered sales, billed amounts or collected revenues. The ideal is to do the grossing up on some measure of physical units billed because the power purchased is measured in physical units. Yet, this may not be feasible where there is incomplete or defective metering among retail customers or the regulator is not able to prevent the company from issuing phantom bills for non-existent customers. As one Indian regulator observed: "There are only two real numbers in the Indian electric sector: purchases and collections. The rest is myth."

This has led to a proposal that the grossing up for allowed losses be performed on actual revenues collected (i.e., monies deposited by the disco in a bank). A difficulty with this approach is that it requires that the revenues be converted into physical units by dividing total revenues by some measure of average tariff. This can become complicated if there is incomplete or inaccurate information of the quantity of electricity sold to each customer class.

The trajectory of loss improvement is also contentious. If the targeted trajectory is too ambitious, private investors may not bid or bid very low. This happened recently in Delhi where the government's privatization proposal set a target of 4 percent loss improvement for each year of an initial, five-year tariff-setting period. Faced with lack of interest from potential bidders, the government eventually agreed to reduce the target to 17 percent over five years when it finally signed a memorandum of understanding with two private companies. The Delhi target is very close to the Uganda government's target of 18 percent reduction in losses over five years. The loss improvement targets in Delhi are relatively low in the first two years but then get much higher in years 4 and 5.

The following are the three most important lessons in designing a multi-year loss target:

1. Once the multi-year loss-reduction target is set, investors must be convinced that the trajectory will remain fixed for the entire tariff-setting period. If they think that the government will readjust (i.e., tighten) the targets within the tariff period, they are not likely to make the investments or take the actions needed to bring down losses.
2. The loss-reduction targets should not require annual measurements because this will inevitably lead to disputes that reduce the regulatory certainty that is being sought in the regulatory contract.
3. The number chosen as the base for grossing up losses must be measured consistently for the entire tariff-setting period.

Second, the new private companies in Latin American generally had the support of local police authorities in collecting from non-paying customers or disconnecting illegal connections. It is questionable whether similar conditions of "law and order" exist in India and Africa.[71] In Orissa, there were allegations that the police prevented employees of the AES-owned distribution company from collecting bills or disconnecting customers. In a letter sent to the Orissa government just before it pulled out, the AES representative asserted that "the lack of law and order support has inhibited the company from undertaking its day-to-day activities such as the collection of dues and the control of the theft of electricity."[72]

The litmus test of whether a government is serious about power sector reform is the day-to-day support that it provides the distribution company to reduce theft. A government must publicly demonstrate an ongoing commitment to basic "law and order" through the passage and enforcement of anti-theft legislation that allows for disconnection and prosecution of those who steal electricity. (Box 6 describes recent efforts in this regard in the Indian State of Andra Pradesh.) A good sign of serious political commitment is if the government successfully prosecutes one or two rich or politically well-connected individuals who have been stealing electricity. The government also needs to pay its own electricity bills. If it fails to take these steps, there is little point in trying to create a regulatory contract, or at least a regulatory contract that places the total risk of collection on the private company (see Boxes 6 and 7).

Box 6: ANDHRA PRADESH: WHERE THERE'S A WILL, THERE'S A WAY

In 1999, N. Chandrababu Naidu, the Chief Minister of the Indian state of Andhra Pradesh, decided that it would be impossible to privatize the state's power enterprises unless power theft was reduced. With the active encouragement of the Chief Minister, a strict Anti-Theft Law (the first of its kind in India) was passed by the state legislature and went into effect on July 1, 2000. The new law provided for:

- A minimum mandatory punishment of 3 to 60 months imprisonment for the theft of electricity.
- Mandatory financial penalties ranging from a minimum of US$120 to a maximum of US$1,200.
- Residents convicted of stealing electricity would be prohibited from receiving electricity for two years.
- The establishment of special courts and tribunals to quickly try cases under the new law.

Before the law went into effect, AP citizens were given the opportunity to pay back bills and to "regularize" their status (i.e., become legal customers if they were illegally connected or their request for legal service had not been processed). In a state of about 75 million people, about 1.9 million applications were received for "regularization." Once the grace period ended, the law was vigorously enforced. From July 2000 to April 2002, more than 2800 people were arrested for stealing electricity (including 87 utility staff and two members of the legislative assembly). Over an 18-month period, billings for electricity increased by 34 percent and revenues increase by 44 percent (while average tariffs increase by 15 percent). Nevertheless, the state-owned power enterprise still experienced major deficits because even with the increase in collections, a large number of agricultural and domestic consumers continue to be supplied electricity without metering and under tariffs that recovered only a small fraction of the cost to serve them.

---

71. In May 2002, several government officials including a police officer and his wife were held hostage by villagers in the Indian state of Haryanna when they came to collect pending electricity bills.

72. Letter to Chief Secretary, Government of Orissa from AES Orissa Distribution Private Limited, July 25, 2001.

Box 7: When the Gap Is Large

The Latin American approach to tariff-setting for privatized distribution entities has generally been successful. Since the mid-1980s, more than 60 government-owned distribution entities have been privatized. But it may be a mistake to assume that the Latin American approach will work equally well in the poorer countries of South Asia and Africa that are now considering privatization. The biggest difference between Latin America and these other regions is that the starting conditions are not the same. India, for example, is different from Latin America in that:

- The current gap between revenues and costs is larger in India (currently revenues fall short of costs by an average of about 30 to 35 percent among Indian state-owned utilities);
- Indian state governments are not in a position to provide credible guarantees of direct or indirect subsidies while the gap is being closed;
- Most sales of electricity to agriculture are not metered;
- The local police may not support private companies when they try to disconnect non-paying or illegal customers (the "law and order" problem);
- A private operator may have limited control over the composition of its labor force in the critical early years of operation because of government commitments to employee unions.

India, like many poor countries, suffers from the "short blanket problem"—the power's sector's revenues are not currently large enough to cover the costs of generation, transmission and distribution. Given these starting conditions, India as well as other poor countries will probably need to employ a different kind of regulatory contract.

One alternative proposal made in the Indian state of Karnataka is called the "distribution margin" approach. Its three key elements are (1) the private distribution company would be granted "first rights" to the flow of revenues collected from retail customers; (2) certain risks (such as collection risk), traditionally borne by a private company, would be explicitly shared with the government; and (3) the government rather than the private company would bear the risk of paying for bulk power purchases and transmission services because the payment received by the state-owned transco and genco would be a residual. The distribution company would commit to handing over to the government whatever revenues remain after the distribution company takes payment for its distribution margin, which would depend on its success in meeting pre-specified performance targets. Because the residual amount would not be adequate, any remaining shortfalls in payments to the transmission entity and generators would become the government's obligation.

Among government and power sector officials, the initial reaction to the "distribution margin" approach was largely negative. It was not uncommon to hear such comments as: "What is the point of privatizing if we are going to bear so much of the risk?" or "This is no different than the demands of IPP developers to put their payments into escrow accounts" or "The disco will not care about retail tariff levels because its payments are guaranteed."

We think the distribution margin approach is worth exploring further for three reasons. First, it has the flexibility of being consistent with a range of risk allocations despite the fact that the initial proposals in India put most risks on government. And like the Latin American price cap approach, it can be combined with pre-set targets for improvements in losses and quality of service. Second, it could be used for a transition period with a pre-scheduled switchover to a more traditional regulatory contract like the ones used in Latin America. Third, it has the potential to "jump-start" improvements in distribution service that may provide government with the political capital for closing the overall cost-tariff gap. But it will probably not be sustainable unless it is combined with an explicit commitment to raise overall retail tariffs in the state and require that farmers pay more than a token amount of money for their electricity.

Foreign Exchange Risks

> *"The power sector pays dearly for the government's macroeconomic sins."*
>
> —Latin American consultant, 2001

> *"Foreign exchange risk is not a risk but a certainty."*
>
> —Latin American power company official

Convertibility Risk and Exchange-Rate Risk

Distribution companies receive payments from their customers in local currency but often incur costs in hard currencies. This leads to two major risks for private investors. The first risk—*convertibility* risk—is that the government will not give the distribution company access to sufficient foreign exchange to pay for costs incurred in hard currencies.[73] The second risk—*exchange-rate* risk—is that the local currency will lose value relative to hard currencies. If the local currency loses value, the distribution company will find that the revenues it receives from its local customers in local currency will buy smaller and smaller quantities of the foreign exchange needed to pay for imported materials, to make interest payments to foreign lenders or to repatriate profits to its investors. The risk, then, is that the local-currency revenues may no longer be sufficient to cover foreign currency costs. This is not a hypothetical risk. Between 1975 and 1995, the currencies of emerging markets declined by an average of one percent per month relative to the dollar (Gray, 2003). Table 4 shows the actual levels of devaluation experienced by one U.S. power company over two decades of operation in five Latin American countries.

TABLE 4: TRENDS IN FOREIGN EXCHANGE RATES IN SELECTED COUNTRIES WHERE AMERICAN AND FOREIGN POWER HAD SUBSIDIARIES

Country	Currency	US$ exchange rate prevailing at dates of major acquisitions	1943	1950	1960
Argentina	peso	$0.424	$0.247	$0.094	$0.012
Brasil, free	cruceiro	.120	.049	.053	.005
Colombia	peso	.973	.572	.510	.151
México	peso	.499	.206	.116	.080
Venezuela	bolivia	.193	.299	.299	.299

Note: All rates are yearly averages except for the 1960 rates, which are for March 31, 1960.
Source: Gomez-Ibanez (1999).

---

73. The World Bank's Multilateral Investment Guarantee Agency (MIGA) will provide guarantees against currency inconvertibility and transfer restrictions. It does not provide guarantees against currency depreciation. See www.miga.org.

Indexing

Indexing is the most common and transparent way to deal with exchange-rate risk.[74] If the local currency loses value relative to the hard currency, the government allows the disco to increase its tariffs by the amount necessary to cover the costs incurred in hard currencies. In theory, this transfers the risk to the distribution company's consumers. Whether this happens in practice depends critically on the extent of indexing and the frequency of adjustments.

Although indexing tends to work reasonably well if the devaluation is small, it usually breaks down when there is a large, sudden devaluation because, if strictly applied, it would trigger large increases in retail tariffs. Not surprisingly, indexing is controversial. During an October 2002 demonstration against indexing of foreign costs in La Paz Bolivia, one protester said: "It is not fair that the population is ever poorer, while the international companies are ever richer for the same work, just because their rates are dollarized."[75]

What the statement fails to recognize is that consumers will inevitably pay in some other way even if indexing is prohibited or incomplete. If indexing is prohibited, this will discourage domestic and foreign investors from investing in the sector.[76] This, in turn, will eventually hurt consumers through power shortages. Alternatively, if indexing is prohibited but the government has a side agreement to provide investors with access to foreign exchange on subsidized terms, consumers will have to pay higher taxes so that the government can recover the foreign exchange subsidy granted to investors.[77] In the first case, the shortages may not arise for several years so the problem is transferred to some future government. In the second case, the subsidy will be hidden in general taxes rather than being observable in highly visible tariff increases. Both of these alternatives to indexing are appealing to politicians because it replaces the visible with the invisible or it postpones the pain to a later government.

Indexing of Power Purchases

The two major components of cost for any distribution company are power purchases and distribution costs (the cost of sending power over distribution facilities and selling it to end users). Among the Southern Cone countries (Argentina, Brazil and Chile) about 45 percent of final tariffs are attributable to power-purchase costs and 55 percent to distribution costs.[78] However, not all of these costs will be indexed for loss of purchasing power relative to hard currencies.

Within the power-purchase category, the percentage of costs that are indexed for foreign exchange fluctuations ranges from 80 to 100 percent for distribution companies in the Southern Cone. In general, the indexing is keyed to benchmark prices rather than the actual prices paid by the distribution entity. For example, the benchmark in Bolivia are "nodal prices" for energy calculated every six months by a stakeholder committee of the National Dispatch Center—and these

---

74. This is not the only available technique for mitigating this risk. Other possible options include reducing foreign currency expenses as a proportion of total expenses, increasing local currency financing, generating hard currency revenues, buying hedging instruments and obtaining government guarantees for a fixed exchange rate. A fuller discussion of these other techniques will be presented in Wright (2003).

75. BNAmericas, October 2, 2002.

76. It will also discourage investment by domestic investors because they, too, need foreign exchange indexing if they buy equipment or acquire capital from outside the country.

77. Between 1953 and 1961, Rio Light, the American and Canadian owned company that served Rio de Janeiro, was classified as an "essential industry" and therefore "could import equipment, remit interest on foreign debt and transfer profits—all at preferential rates that represented about one-half the cost of exchange to non-preferred sectors." The advantage of subsidizing the exchange rate was that it "provided a less politically sensitive way of returning to the company roughly what the artificially low power rates took away." Tendler (1968).

78. In India, the proportions are quite different. For a typical Indian distribution entity, about 75 percent of the final tariffs are attributable to power-purchase costs and 25 percent to distribution costs. The higher proportion of power-purchase costs reflects the fact that Indian distribution entities have to buy more power to make up for high levels of theft and that the power they purchase is more expensive because they generally lack access to large quantities of hydro power or low-cost natural gas.

prices must be approved by the regulator. The nodal price is an estimate of the short run marginal cost of supplying at different nodes on the system. Between calculations, the nodal price is 90 percent indexed to changes in the price of gas (which, in turn, are linked to a dollar index) and 10 percent to an index of local inflation. There is a different weighting for energy capacity payments—70 percent is tied to the U.S. dollar exchange rate and 30 percent to local inflation. The adjustments for both energy and capacity are made monthly. The details of the indexing arrangements are written into Bolivian law, which makes the indexing more certain from an investor's perspective.

Brazil uses a different type of benchmark. As discussed earlier, until early 2002, indexing was applied to *valores normativos* (VN), which are the regulator's estimates of the long-run marginal cost of generating electricity from different fuels and technologies. Each distributor must file with ANEEL the proposed long-term contract it wishes to sign. ANEEL reviews the contract to make sure the percentage of foreign exchange indexing does not exceed its guidelines. Once the contract is accepted, it receives a VN value that is indexed over the life of the contract. In the case of natural-gas–fired units, about 75 percent of the VN value is indexed to the dollar and 25 percent to local inflation. The decision on the appropriate weights is made by the regulator on a case-by-case basis and ANEEL is allowed to change the weights after ten years and then after every five years.

Unlike Bolivia, Chile and Peru, Brazil has a significant lag in the indexed adjustments because Brazilian law specifies that indexing can be performed only once a year in any contract. In October 2001, the regulations were changed to allow the distribution companies to charge interest for the time value of money lost between the yearly adjustments (see Box 3 in Chapter 5). More recently, there have been public discussions of replacing the VN system with power-purchase price caps keyed to the outcome of a mandated competitive procurement requirement for distribution companies or some other market benchmarks. If this change were made, then the foreign exchange adjustment mechanism would no longer be administratively determined but would be the outcome of a competitive procurement process or a specified market benchmark.

Indexing of Distribution Costs
The level of foreign exchange indexing is lower for distribution costs than for power costs. This reflects the fact that a higher proportion of distribution costs are incurred locally. Peru and Chile allow about 12 to 17 percent of distribution costs to be indexed to the dollar; this is roughly the percentage of capital costs within overall distribution costs. Neither Brazil nor Bolivia allows any indexing of distribution costs to the dollar. Instead, they provide for indexing that is tied to one or more measures of domestic inflation rather than to a foreign exchange index.

However, even an index that ostensibly measures just local inflation may, in fact, be heavily influenced by foreign exchange fluctuations. This seems to be the case in Brazil. The concession contract of most Brazilian distribution companies provides that distribution costs will be indexed to a Brazilian price index known as the IGPM that is significantly affected by foreign exchange fluctuations. About 50 percent of the distribution companies overall costs is comprised of distribution costs, while the other 50 percent is largely attributable to the cost of power purchases. Within the distribution cost category, it has been estimated that about 80 percent of the costs are wages and salaries. In 2002, there was almost no inflation in Brazilian wages and salaries but the IGPM index increased by about 20 to 28 percent.

Brazilian consumers and government officials have argued that that it is unfair for distribution companies to be allowed to increase the entire distribution cost component of their retail tariffs by 20 to 28 percent when the actual inflation in distribution costs was much lower. However, this criticism ignores the fact that the phenomenon is cyclical. In other periods, the foreign exchange rate may be stable, while domestic inflation is increasing. During these periods, the IGPM index will fail to reflect inflation in distribution costs. Although the ideal would be to use an index that is more closely correlated to actual distribution cost changes (whether caused by

TABLE 5: INCREASE IN END-USER TARIFFS ARISING FROM DIFFERENT LEVELS OF INDEXING FOR FOREIGN EXCHANGE FLUCTUATIONS (%)

Proportion of costs that are indexed	10% Devaluation	50% Devaluation	100% Devaluation	300% Devaluation
20%	2%	10%	20%	60%
50%	5%	25%	50%	150%
100%	10%	50%	100%	300%

domestic inflation or foreign exchange depreciation), such indexes do not exist in most developing countries.[79]

Adjustment of distribution costs can also occur in other ways. In most Southern Cone countries regulators recalculate the distribution rate base at the end of a four-to-seven–year tariff period using an estimate of reproduction cost rather than historic cost. Because the calculation is based on an estimate of a new, optimized distribution network to serve the distribution company's particular configuration, the effect of foreign exchange depreciation will be picked up in the calculation if the optimized network includes the use of imported equipment. This leads to a larger rate base that, in turn, produces higher tariffs.

The Special Case of Argentina

Until recently, Argentina has been an exception to the Latin American rule because of its over-indexing to the dollar. For the three privately owned distribution companies in Buenos Aires regulated by the national electricity regulator, *all costs*, whether incurred domestically or overseas, were indexed to the U.S. dollar until early 2002. (In contrast, only about 40 to 50 percent of end-user tariffs are indexed to the dollar in other Southern Cone countries.) This left Argentina vulnerable when the Argentine peso experienced a major devaluation relative to the dollar in late 2001. (See Table 5 for a simulation of the relationship between end-user tariff increases and percentage of costs that are covered by foreign exchange indices.) If the tariff formula had been applied as specified, the devaluation would have triggered increases of about 300 percent in retail electricity tariffs.

This never happened, however, because in January 2002 the Argentine government enacted a law that prohibited the continued usage of such formulas. The law stated that "any dollar index or other foreign currency index clause or any foreign countries price index provided for in any contracts signed by the Public Administration is declared null and void from the enactment of this Act...."[80] As this is being written, negotiations are under way to replace these indices with some other mechanism; however, it remains unclear what the new system will be and how it will affect future foreign investment in the power sector.

79. In France, the law "expressly forbids the linking of any contract to the consumer price index, to 'the general level of prices or salaries,' or to 'prices or goods or services having no relation to the objective of [the contract] or to the activity of one of the parties.'" Shugart (1998), p. 111.

80. Some private investors argue that the January 2002 law does not affect the indexing provisions in their concession agreements. They contend that it only repeals a 1991 peso-dollar convertibility law and cannot nullify indexing provisions in specific contracts. This legal argument has yet to be tested in Argentine courts.

Obligation to Supply

Obligation to serve goes by different names. In some common law countries, it is referred to as the *supply obligation*. In civil code countries, it is usually described as a *public service obligation*. In most developing countries, the state-owned utility has always had a public service obligation. This legal obligation usually flowed from the fact that supply of electricity was defined as a "public service" (i.e., an obligation of the state) in the country's constitution.[81] As one Indian regulator observed, however, such requirements were often nothing more than "pretty poetry" because state enterprises rarely achieved what was required of them.

The reasons for failure have been well documented: lack of money, ongoing political interference in operating and investment decisions and, perhaps most important, lack of incentives (World Bank, 1995). The last point simply refers to the fact that most officials in publicly owned power enterprises do not earn higher salaries if they succeed or lose their jobs if they fail. In contrast, the public service obligation of a private distribution company is viewed as real and enforceable. When a private company takes over, one Indian government official observed that "excuses are no longer acceptable and good performance is expected from Day 1."

Toward a Precise Definition

In designing the regulatory contract for the new private owner, a key design question is: what should be the specific elements of the obligation to serve? In most countries, it is generally accepted that the loose "universal public service obligation" that was adequate for the state enterprise (probably because it was neither contested nor enforced) will have to be replaced with a more precise definition of obligation to serve for private companies. The new definition must answer the following questions:

- Who must be served?
- What are the initial and phased in technical and commercial standards for service?
- What are the penalties if the company fails to meet these standards?
- Are excuses allowed?

The regulatory contract, whether it is a concession or a license, has to give clear answers to these questions.[82]

Starting Points Matter

The definition of obligation to serve cannot and should not be the same across all countries. A system's starting conditions must be considered in defining an appropriate obligation. Among the more important starting points are the size of the revenue-cost gap, the extent of electrification, and adequacy of overall installed generation capacity. These starting conditions, in turn, affect the two key dimensions of obligation to serve: geographic scope and whether the obligation is absolute or conditional.

---

81. In developed countries, the public service obligation is defined more broadly than the obligation to supply. An Italian electricity regulator stated that the public service obligation in his country had four elements: universal service, security of supply, environmental protection and promotion of competition. Available at www.iea.org/about/forum/garribba.pdf.

82. In India, one criticism of the Delhi government's privatization proposal was that the privatization package did not contain a proposed license so that bidders do not know the extent of their legal obligation to serve. In contrast, most other Indian states (Haryanna, Andhra Pradesh, Uttar Pradesh and Karnataka) that are contemplating privatization have issued detailed licenses for their government-owned distribution entities that give potential bidders a clearer idea of the service obligations that will be expected of them.

Geographic Scope

In most developed countries, a distribution company's obligation to serve is typically defined relative to a specific geographic area. Within this area, the company is obligated to connect every potential customer and provide retail customers with the same quality of service—unless a customer chooses to pay more for a higher level of service or less for a lower level (for example, paying less if the company has the right to interrupt with notice for a certain number of times during the year).

However, this universal obligation to serve is generally not feasible in developing countries where there is less than full electrification. This is explicitly recognized in many Latin American countries, where the typical concession agreement often distinguishes a company's obligation to serve depending on the potential customer's location relative to existing distribution facilities. The concession agreement may require that the company connect any potential customer within 100 meters of an existing distribution facility, grant first right of supply but not an obligation to serve for potential customers between 100 and 500 meters, and impose no obligation at all if the customer is located more than 500 meters from an existing distribution facility. Within the first band of 100 meters, the company is usually obligated to connect customers for a pre-specified "regulated" connection charge. Beyond this first band, the company is generally permitted to charge customers a connection fee based on the company's actual costs. (See Appendix B for a similar approach proposed in a South Asian country.) This approach reflects the broader policy decision that the government rather than the private company will be responsible for rural electrification.

A company's obligation to serve may be further qualified by the condition that the company is not obligated to provide a customer with electric service unless it can recover the costs of serving that customer. For example, a concession or license may specify that a company is not obligated to connect a new customer unless it receives payment for some or all of the capital costs of connection from the customer, the government, or a combination of the two. This is the regulatory regime in Guatemala and Chile. In Guatemala, the government has used the proceeds of privatization to create a fund to subsidize the cost of interconnecting new poor rural customers. The private company receives the capital cost subsidy only after the connection is made and is found to satisfy pre-specified technical standards.[83] In Chile, the government provides subsidies for both the capital costs and operating costs to serve poor rural customers.[84] The subsidy does not come for free. The government will not pay the subsidy unless the customer pays his part of the bill. Therefore, in both of these countries the obligation to serve new customers is a limited rather than a universal obligation. Specifically, the obligation to connect and supply new customers is contingent upon payment of a subsidy by government.

Absolute or Limited Obligation?

When Argentina initiated its privatization process in 1992, it imposed an absolute obligation to serve on the three new private distribution companies that served metropolitan Buenos Aires. The concession agreements required the distribution companies to provide service to all customers within their service areas even if there was an "upstream" failure by generators or the system operator. This is, in effect, an absolute, "no excuses" obligation to serve. One advantage of this approach is that the regulator does not need to sort out who was responsible for the failure because the distribution company is always held accountable. Yet, it is a feasible standard only if a country has close to an adequate supply of generation at the time of privatization.

---

83. Harris (2002).

84. For example, in August 2000 the government of the Bolivian Department of Cochabamba sought bids from private developers to extend electrical service to 380 unserved rural communities. The bidders bid the right to receive a one-time capital cost subsidy from various local governments. The winning bidder, ELEFEC, received a subsidy payment of US$7.3 million or 90 percent of the total capital costs of US$8.1 million.

It makes little sense to impose an absolute obligation to serve on newly privatized distribution companies in countries that are starting from a base of insufficient available generating capacity or inadequate transmission capacity to transport the electricity back to the distribution system. This situation arose in the case of Telasi, the AES distribution company that was serving the capital city of Tbilisi. During the winter of 2001, Tbilisi experienced many hours of blackouts. The regulatory commission announced that it would penalize Telasi for a failure to supply even though the regulatory contract within the privatization agreement seemed to specify a "best-efforts standard." Telasi protested and threatened to leave the country.[85] Among other things, it argued that it was the only distribution company in the country to have paid "hard cash" to generators. It also contended that its failure to supply was caused, at least in part, by the fact that about 25 percent of the power that it had paid for had been diverted by the government-controlled system operator to non-paying, state-owned distribution entities.[86]

Without judging the merits of AES arguments, it appears that in countries where there is inadequate generation supply, it is unreasonable and counterproductive for a government to impose an absolute obligation to serve on new distribution companies. During the initial post-privatization years, the standard has to be a conditional, best-efforts obligation. In practice, this means a standard that includes some or all of the following elements:

> The company should use all reasonable efforts to provide energy and related services to customers 24 hours per day using Good Utility Practice provided that the company is allowed to charge customers the cost of providing that service or the government makes timely subsidy payments for any shortfall between the cost of serving the customer and the tariffs that can be charged that customer. Moreover, the company shall not be liable for any failure of the company to supply energy that arises from (a) a fault or failure of any part of the network that could not have been prevented by Good Utility Practice (taking into account the state of the network that existed on the date of this agreement); or (b) the failure of any energy supplier, transmission company, system operator to generate, transmit and/or dispatch energy; or (c) any Force Majeure event.[87]

Quality of Service

Although it is counterproductive to try to impose quality-of-service standards that cannot be met, this does not mean that quality of service should be ignored. Unfortunately, although everyone talks about improving quality of service, in practice technical and commercial quality of service receive very little attention in most distribution privatizations. This happens because it is much easier to specify tariff rules than quality-of-service standards. Basic electricity laws usually make only general references to quality of service. And because quality of service gets little attention, consumers often associate distribution privatizations with "higher tariffs and nothing else." The danger in ignoring quality of service is that the political support that exists for privatization will soon disappear in the absence of some "early wins" on quality of service. As one high level Indian government official observed, "We can fight the political battles if the supply is good."

---

85. The same issue arose in New Delhi when there were widespread blackouts four days after the government-owned system had been privatized. A high level executive in one of the new private distribution companies was quoted as saying that the "private Companies have only taken over the distribution of power not the transmission. We are only able to distribute the power that we receive." "India's Power Privatization Leaves New Delhi Blacked Out," *The Times of India*, July 05, 2002.

86. AES Press Release at www.aes-telasi.com/news.htm.

87. From a draft of a proposed distribution license in an East Asian country considering privatization of distribution.

Appendix C presents a proposed regulatory framework for establishing quality-of-service standards developed for a South Asian country. The framework is based on the following principles:

■ Quality-of-service standards should be established for those dimensions of service that are important to consumers, controllable by the licensee and capable of being measured on a reasonably objective basis.

■ Quality-of-service standards need not be uniform across all customer categories or geographic areas. The standards should be based on customers' preferences and their willingness to pay for the costs of providing the specified level of quality. Quality-of-service costs money. The regulator should not impose quality-of service standards on a distribution company unless its customers are willing and able to pay for the costs associated with meeting the standards.

■ Quality-of-service standards should be established for both technical and commercial dimensions of service. The quality-of-service standards may be (1) guaranteed standards where the standard must be achieved in all specified cases and (2) overall standards where the standard must be achieved on average across a specified customer category but need not be satisfied for all customers in the category.

■ Quality-of-service standards and associated penalties and rewards should be phased in over time. Any penalties should be related to the disutility experienced by the customer and the costs likely to be incurred by the distribution entity in meeting the standards.

■ Where it is feasible and efficient, penalties should be paid to individual consumers. Otherwise, penalties should be used to provide subsidies to poor customers. Penalties should not be used to support the budget of the regulator or any other government entity. Penalties and rewards should be capped so that they do not exceed more than 2 to 4 percent of the distribution entity's overall revenues.

■ Any changes in quality-of-service standards should be synchronized with the regulatory proceeding to update tariffs for a new multi-year period.

■ The regulatory entity should have the legal authority to delegate quality-of-service monitoring and the imposition of penalties to a third party. However, the regulatory entity has ultimate responsibility for ensuring compliance even if it chooses to delegate to a third party.

■ The regulatory entity should establish a reliable, objective and publicly available monitoring system that compares the quality of service provided by different distribution entities.[88]

Extend the Obligation to Generators?

In most countries where there has been unbundling (i.e., vertical separation), the obligation to serve, whether absolute or conditional, remains exclusively with the distribution entity.[89] One exception is Chile. Following three major droughts that led to rationing, the Chilean government in 1999 modified the existing electricity law to impose an obligation to serve on existing and future generators to serve certain regulated customers or compensate them for failure to supply (i.e., failure payments) even if the failure was caused by drought. In other words, drought would no longer be defined as a *force majeure* for hydro generators.

It appears that the imposition of this "extra-contractual" obligation to serve, when combined with the risk of "failure payments," has made Chile too risky a place to invest for generators. Even if one concluded that it is equitable and efficient to impose the drought risk on generators,

---

88. For a good overview of quality of service regulation, see Foster (1999).

89. For example, Article 2 of the Bolivian Electricity Law defines the electrical output of generators as a "commodity." The rationale for this designation was to make it clear that generators did not have any obligation to serve beyond what they voluntarily agree to in privately negotiated contracts.

such a policy will be unworkable unless generators are explicitly allowed to recover the expected costs of making "failure payments" to their customers in times of drought. But the current Chilean system fixes a ceiling price that generators can charge distributors which is limited to the regulator's estimate of nodal (i.e., location-specific marginal) costs. The nodal price has no explicit provision for recovering the expected cost of "failure payments." Therefore, it should not be surprising that generators are reluctant to build new facilities to serve the incremental needs of Chilean distributors.[90]

Faced with a looming energy shortage, the government has proposed a "solution" that would give it the authority to order the system operator to conduct a competitive procurement for new thermal generation whenever the expected supply is deemed inadequate to serve demand during the next 30 months. The problem with this "solution" is that it leads to more government intervention and does not address the fundamental problem: imposing an obligation to serve on generators without any provision to compensate them for the cost of meeting this obligation. The basic lesson is that legal obligations impose costs and the costs must be recoverable in tariffs or there will be insufficient investment.

---

90. As *Business News Americas* reported, "This is Chilectra's [a distribution company] fourth attempt to contract a 400–gigawatt-hour supply. Previous attempts were abandoned because no bids were received from generators, who are reluctant to take on new commitments with distributors while they are under the obligation to compensate interruptions in supply whatever the reason, including during drought." Bnamericas.com, "Chilectra extends tender deadlines," April 12, 2002.

CHAPTER 6

DEALING WITH DISPUTES

"Nearly a decade after Beijing opened its doors to foreign investment in the power sector, the industry is littered with the remains of foreign investments wrecked by renegotiated or reinterpreted pricing agreements."

—*Far Eastern Economic Review*, January 31, 2002

"The inability of societies to develop effective, low-cost enforcement of contracts is the most important source of both historical stagnation and contemporary underdevelopment in the Third World."

—Douglas C. North, Nobel Laureate and author of *Institutions, Institutional Change and Economic Performance* (1990)

A distribution utility can be involved in many disputes. The three principal types of disputes are those between the distribution company and its customers, between the distribution company and other industry participants, and between the distribution company and its regulator. Our focus here is on the last type—disputes between the distribution and the regulator over either the substance of the regulator's decisions or the process by which the regulator reached these decisions.

Who Regulates the Regulator?

Independence is not infallibility. The fact that a regulator has been given some degree of legal independence does not mean that the regulator will always make the right decision. Thus there must be some mechanism to review the regulator's decisions. This is not easy because the almost universal reality is that regulators do not like their decisions to be reviewed.[91]

---

91. In an exception to the rule, one former Sri Lankan regulator observed that "...appeals are necessary. It is a discipline that we need because we are exercising discretion." Samarajiva (2001).

If there is a mandated mechanism of review, most new regulators in developing countries would prefer that the review take place in a regular court of law. This preference probably reflects the fact that most courts will generally review challenges only on points of law or the process by which a regulator arrived at a decision, rather than the substance of the decision itself. And because a regulator is usually able to avoid making a procedural or legal mistake (especially if the agency has created its own procedures), a regulator knows that he or she is more likely to win if the dispute goes to a traditional court. Regulators also know that a regular court will probably take several years to render a decision. So even if the decision is in favor of the licensee and against the regulator, it will effectively be in favor of the regulator because the court decision may no longer be useful to the company by the time it is issued.

Given these realities, it is not surprising that international investors are becoming increasingly reluctant to invest in electricity distribution unless regulatory disputes are dealt with outside the regular court system. Many dispute resolution mechanisms have been developed for infrastructure contracts where a government enterprise is the buyer. The question, then, is: Are these dispute resolution mechanisms equally applicable to regulatory disputes?

What Gets Disputed?

No regulatory contract can be totally clear or perfectly capable of anticipating future events. As one observer of U.S. regulation has commented, "at the edges of words there are always interpretations" (Howard, 1996). And even if there are no ambiguities in the contract at the time it was signed, the two parties will never be able to predict everything that might happen. Or, in the worst case, one of the two parties is no longer able willing or able to comply with the contract. It is thus inevitable that there will be disputes between new private distribution companies and the government or regulator even where there has been a concerted effort to "contractualize" the entire tariff-setting system.[92]

In countries that have recently privatized distribution, disputes have arisen over the following:

- The extent of pass-through of taxes (Georgia).
- The calculation of benchmarks for the pass-through of the costs of power purchases (Brazil).
- The reimbursement for lost revenues because of government-mandated rationing (Brazil).
- The responsibility for blackouts and brownouts caused by non-performance of generators and system operators (Georgia).
- The process for adjusting tariffs to reflect the cost of new distribution investments (Georgia).
- The disallowance of about 30 percent of the distribution company's new investments (Moldova).
- The methodology for calculating the asset base for setting tariffs in subsequent multi-year periods (Brazil).
- The tightening of a loss-reduction target by the regulator that had been contractually fixed in the tariff methodology specified in the privatization agreement (Moldova).
- Whether rates of return in subsequent multi-year periods should be calculated on a uniform or company-by-company basis (Colombia).
- The allowed technical and commercial loss levels and allowed operating and maintenance costs in subsequent multi-year periods (Colombia).

---

92. Our focus will be on disputes involving the regulator and the distribution company. Disputes between the distribution company and its customers and between the distribution company and other industry participants will not be discussed.

Given the inevitability of disputes, it critical that any attempt at regulation by contract be accompanied by a dispute resolution system that has the confidence of both government and investors.[93] An effective dispute resolution system must include three principal elements:

1. The means of dispute resolution,
2. The types of relief that can be given (such as tariff adjustments, cost pass-throughs, damages, specific changes to regulatory rules, injunctions and orders for specific performance), and
3. A mechanism to ensure that the decision will be honored in a timely manner.[94]

Different Approaches to Dispute Resolution

The various approaches to resolving disputes include the following:

- The local court system
- International arbitration
- Mediation
- Expert panels
- A specialized appeals tribunal.

The Local Court System

In an ideal world, any dispute between the licensee and the regulator would go to a local court that makes a decision in "an informed, sophisticated and low-cost way" (Williamson, 1983). In many developing countries, however, the local court system rarely exhibits these qualities. At best, local courts are slow. At worst, they are corrupt. And it is almost inevitable that they will have an inherent bias in favor of local interests, consumers and institutions.

In addition, traditional local courts are likely to exhibit two other weaknesses when confronted with regulatory disputes. First, the courts may not be knowledgeable about the technical, engineering and financial issues that underlie the disputes. Second, even if the judges happen to have the necessary knowledge, they may still be limited by law or precedent to examining whether there was compliance with the regulatory process rather than examining the substance of the decision.[95] Generally, this means that the court's review will be limited to examining whether the regulator

- acted outside the scope of its powers,
- did not follow the procedures that it was obliged to follow,
- breached procedural due process or acted unfairly,
- acted unreasonably, or
- made an error of fact or law.

---

93. In the Lamech and Saeed (2003) survey, about 45 percent of the investors that responded said that "the fair adjudication of tariff adjustments and disputes" was a critical to the success or failure of their power sector investment.

94. A good general discussion of the strengths and weaknesses of various dispute resolution mechanisms can be found in Kerf (1998).

95. For example, the Indian Supreme Court, in reviewing the decision of a state High Court, made the following observation: "All that the High Court has to be satisfied with is that the Commission has followed the proper procedure and unless it can be demonstrated that its decisions is on the face of it arbitrary or illegal or contrary to the Act, the Court will not interfere." Supreme Court of India, (2002) 3 Supreme Court Cases 711, "Association of Industrial Electricity Users versus State of AP and Others," March 6, 2002.

The propensity for deciding regulatory disputes on narrow legal or process grounds is not a phenomenon unique to developing countries. In both developed and developing countries, the traditional standard of judicial review for appeals of a regulator's decision "does not allow the court to review the merits of the decision itself; instead, the court can only review the merits of the manner in which the decision was made" (Lawrence, 2002; Green, 1999).

Limiting a legal review to "process" is generally not very comforting to private investors. From an investor's perspective, it is especially frustrating if a court upholds a regulator's decisions because the regulator followed all the correct procedures but the substantive decision was patently absurd. And even if the investor "wins" because the regulator made a procedural or legal mistake, a court is generally not allowed to change the regulator's initial decision. Instead, the court can only set aside the regulator's decision and order the regulator to reconsider the matter. So the "victory" for the private investor may be more theoretical than real. Given these typical conditions, most private foreign investors understandably want access to a dispute resolution system that examines the substance of the regulator's decision more than the process by which it is arrived at.

International Arbitration

The term *arbitration* usually refers to a dispute resolution mechanism whereby the disputing parties submit their disputes to a non-judicial body that has the power to make decisions that are binding on the parties. International investors almost always prefer international (i.e., out-of-country) arbitration for disputes.[96] International arbitration usually takes place in another country but with an obligation placed upon local courts to enforce the foreign award as provided for under the terms of an international treaty or convention. Private investors prefer international arbitration because they consider it to be neutral, there are good procedural rules for the parties to present their case, and it is likely to produce the fairest result (at least from their perspective). If adopted, arbitration can be invoked at the initiative of either party. It is increasingly the norm in infrastructure contracts in which a private foreign investor builds or operates a facility that produces an output or service purchased by a government-owned entity.

Who Is Appointed and What Do They Do?

The arbitrators (typically one or three) can be appointed by agreement between the parties or, if the parties cannot agree, by an independent and neutral institution such as the International Chamber of Commerce (ICC), the International Centre for Settlement of Investment Disputes or a Bar Association. In some countries, an arbitration association has been established and funded by all the players in that country for the express purpose of establishing a common set of rules for arbitration of disputes arising from contracts in that country and the appointment of suitably qualified arbitrators.

Panel members can also be appointed before any dispute arises. For example, some contracts for major infrastructure development (such as IPP projects) have included provisions where a panel of three arbitrators who are well respected by the parties and who have first-class international experience and reputations can be appointed before any dispute arises. The advantage of creating a standing expert panel is that the panel can be used for other forms of dispute resolution that may eliminate the need for formal arbitration.[97]

---

96. For a detailed study of national or within-country arbitration applied to regulatory disputes involving water concessions in Manila, see Houston and Bowley (2000).

97. Another advantage is that the panel will be ready to hear disputes as soon as one party makes a formal notification. In the previously cited Manila Water Concession arbitration system, it took six months to find three individuals to serve on the panel after the company filed a formal request for arbitration. See Houston and Bowley (2000), p. 20.

In addition to adjudication of the dispute through formal arbitration, the panel can also be used for a less formal process designed to minimize the need for formal arbitrations. For example, the panel can be asked to give a preliminary view or report on the facts as presented to them (see below). This finding of fact, because it is made by a panel of well respected and experienced individuals, can be prepared quickly and is a powerful tool for the parties to use to settle the dispute. In effect, the panel is available to serve two functions: first, as an expert fact-finding panel and second, as an arbitration panel.

Although this technique has been largely limited to infrastructure projects where a government entity is the buyer rather than the regulator, there is no obvious reason why the same technique could not be used for regulatory contracts. To make it workable for regulatory contracts, it would be necessary, because of the duration of the regulatory contract, to include a mechanism for replacing an arbitrator who, for whatever reason, became unavailable. In fact, recent proposals in several countries would create special electricity or infrastructure tribunals (see below) that operate outside of or as a complement to regular courts. Such tribunals are, in effect, an attempt to create something akin to a standing panel of experts. There is one important difference between the two proposals, however: whereas both the government and the distribution company would jointly determine the members of the panel of experts, the government alone would determine the membership of the special tribunal. For this reason, most international investors will probably prefer an expert panel over an appellate tribunal.

The Arbitration Rules

The arbitration rules are an important ingredient for international arbitration. Very few contract parties make up the rules and attach them to the agreement (although this was done in the case of Channel Tunnel concession). Instead, they usually incorporate well established international rules such as those developed by the International Chamber of Commerce (ICC), the London Court of Arbitration (LCIA) or the U.N. Commission on International Trade Law (UNCITRAL). Although in a strict legal sense a regulatory contract may be signed by only two parties (the government and the company), consumers are obviously an important shadow party to the contract. Therefore, if international arbitration is included in a regulatory contract, it may be necessary to modify the existing process rules to provide the appropriate mechanics for an arbitration involving three or more parties.

Pendulum Arbitration

Some contracts contain what is called a "pendulum" or "baseball" provision. This provision limits the scope of the arbitrators to impose their own solutions, which might be different from either of those sought by the contract parties.[98] The pendulum provision limits the arbitrator to choosing a solution or relief sought by one of the parties. The arbitrator is not allowed to choose a solution of his or her own crafting. Pendulum arbitration is usually proposed to protect the parties from idiosyncratic decision-making by the arbitrator. It also promotes the prospects of an amicable settlement by forcing each party to present a more reasonable position to the arbitrator. Where there is pendulum arbitration, the two disputing parties will tend not to propose extreme positions because doing so increases the risk that the arbitrator will choose the other party's position. Its principal disadvantage is that it can limit the arbitrator's ability to make decisions that represent a fair compromise to the interests of the parties and, perhaps, a better solution for the future, given the long-term nature of the contract.

---

98. It is described as *baseball arbitration* in the United States because it is often used in salary disputes between baseball players and the baseball club's management. The arbitrator must select one of the two proposed salaries and is prohibited from choosing any other values (such as splitting the difference in the proposed salaries).

Pendulum arbitration has been proposed in Chile for tariff disputes involving distribution utilities. At present, the Chilean regulatory contract provides that distribution tariffs are reset every four years based on a weighted average of the tariff values proposed by consultants for the regulator and the distribution companies. Not surprisingly, this system has created incentives for the regulator's consultant to produce a low number and the companies' consultant to produce a high number. With each successive tariff-setting exercise, the tariffs proposed by the two sides have come to diverge by ever larger amounts. In an attempt to get more-reasonable estimates from the regulator and the companies, it has been proposed that the law be modified so that in the future an arbitrator (perhaps taking the form of a special economic tribunal) is required to choose only of the two presented values.

Enforcement of Arbitration Awards

Enforcement will be a major concern with the design of any international arbitration system for a regulatory contract. Much will depend on the law of the jurisdiction in which the arbitration award must be enforced. The New York Convention on the Recognition and Enforcement of Foreign Arbitral Awards is designed to provide a mechanism for the automatic enforcement of arbitration awards in the countries that are parties to the Convention. However, there are examples where local laws have been in conflict (either inadvertently or deliberately) with the letter or spirit of the convention, making it very difficult for international investors to enforce arbitration awards. For example, many countries that are signatories to international arbitration conventions reserve the right to limit "the application of an award to differences arising out of legal relationships that are considered as commercial under the national law of the enforcing state" (Houston and Bowley, 2000). Unless the initial agreement is drawn tightly, a regulatory commission whose decision is overturned or modified could, after the fact, argue that the arbitration panel's decision is unenforceable because it raises overriding constitutional or policy considerations.

Criticisms of International Arbitration

International arbitration under international rules has been criticized on several grounds. Government officials in developing countries do not like international arbitration because they view it as an affront to their national dignity. In particular, they consider it as an attack on their legal sovereignty. Some countries have directly or indirectly prohibited its use. Just as international investors believe that they will not receive impartial and timely justice in a local court system, government officials in developing countries believe (rightly or wrongly) that international arbitration will always tend to favor the foreign private investors. As a consequence, it is not surprising that they view "international arbitration as a foreign institution imposed upon them with a heavy Western bias" (Schwartz and Paulson, 1999). Nevertheless, international arbitration has become widely used because it is the *quid pro quo* for access to international financing.

Even practitioners of international arbitration recognize that it has problems. They will usually admit that arbitration is often no simpler than litigation because it requires rules of procedure to cover all eventualities and to ensure that the proceedings are fair, to allow the parties to state their cases fully and to be heard. It is also recognized that arbitration can be as lengthy as court proceedings (although it may not involve waiting for long periods before hearings can be scheduled). Finally, it can be as expensive as litigation (and sometimes more expensive), particularly if the case is complex.

In our view, international arbitration is a necessary and appropriate backstop for regulatory disputes in countries with no track record for impartial resolution of such disputes. That said, it is best held in reserve as a last resort for dealing with disputes. Its principal value is derived from the simple fact that it exists, even if it is never used. The mere fact that it is available to both parties will often act as an inducement for the parties to settle. It becomes particularly effective if it is not a stand-alone option, but is combined with other forms of dispute resolution (such as an expert panel) that are faster and less costly to use. When international arbitration is packaged with other forms of dispute resolution, smaller disputes are less likely to grow into big disputes.

Mediation

Another alternative to adjudication in a local court or international arbitration is Alternative Dispute Resolution (ADR). ADR has developed in many countries in order to meet the criticisms of the length and cost of litigation and arbitration and, perhaps, to a lesser extent, to meet concerns over the unsatisfactory nature of the outcomes in some cases. ADR typically involves the facilitation of structured efforts (for example, expert panels and mediation) by the parties to settle dispute for themselves without going to a local court.

Mediation is the most common form of ADR. It involves the appointment of an experienced mediator or mediation team that carries out a process designed to enable the parties to better understand each other's concerns and positions and to negotiate a settlement or agreement on a mutual-gains basis. The mediator may be empowered or mandated to seek a negotiated outcome that is acceptable to the parties. When it works well, mediation or any other form of voluntary ADR can produce a better answer for the contract parties, if they take full ownership. It has been successfully used in regulatory adjudication and rule-making proceedings in the U.S.[99]

However, because of its informal nature, the mediation process does not impose any resolution or decision upon the parties. There will be no binding resolution of the dispute unless and until an agreement is reached and committed to writing at the end of the ADR process. Moreover, a party is free to walk away from the process at any time up to that point. The success of ADR thus depends on the willingness of the parties to make the process work, or on their being persuaded, often by the mediation team, that the process could or should be made to work. Where there is more than two parties to the dispute or the issues are complex, this can be a particular challenge.

Any settlement that is reached is, by definition, outside of the contract terms. The question therefore arises of how such an agreement can be enforced. The regulatory contract or the enabling legislation could provide that all settlements reached as a result of mediation or some other form of ADR be subject to revisions to the contract that will be fully implemented by the parties. However, this may deter the parties from using ADR (if they have the choice). ADR works best where parties enter into the process willingly in the hope that they will reach a settlement.

Several distribution concessions in Brazil contain provisions for mediation of disputes with the regulator. For example, the concession agreement for AES Sul provides for the establishment of a committee of three specialists with the responsibility for "suggesting...[a] negotiated solution for the conflict."[100] There is, however, a fundamental problem with the Brazilian mediation approach. In general, the mediation panel can be convened only if the two parties, the regulator and the aggrieved distribution company, both agree to convene the panel. But it is highly unlikely that the regulator will voluntarily agree to enter into dispute resolution because this would be equivalent to admitting that he or she may have made a mistake. Regulators, like most human beings, are generally reluctant to admit to mistakes—especially if it weakens the regulator's legal position if there is a later formal appeal to a regular court.

In Brazil, the panels are further limited by the fact that they can only "suggest" (in effect, mediate) a solution. Even if a distribution company could require that a panel be convened, this will not accomplish very much if the regulator is an unwilling party to the mediation. A regulatory dispute is different from a commercial dispute because in a commercial dispute both the buyer and seller will usually have an economic incentive to resolve the dispute. This is not true for regulatory disputes.

---

99. Raab (1994). These proceedings have generally been used to negotiate a prospective agreement between a company and its customers or to develop a consensus on a proposed new rule covering technical issues for which the regulator may have limited expertise. If the regulator agrees with the negotiated "settlement," he may formally approve it. The U.S. FERC has made extensive use of ADR for these types of proceedings. See www.ferc.fed.us/public/adr.pdf. In general, ADR in the United States has *not* been used to mediate disputes between the regulator and an affected company once the regulator has issued a formal order on the matter.

100. Distribution Concession Agreement 12/97, Article 15.

In general, regulators will have no incentive to agree to mediation or other forms of voluntary ADR. Although a government could try to pressure the regulator to enter into negotiation, such pressures could put the government in the awkward position of being seen as trying to compromise the regulator's independence.

Expert Panels

Expert panels have been used as a means of resolving disputes, on either an interim or a final basis, in some infrastructure contracts. The members of the panel are chosen for their experience and understanding of the issues. The perceived advantage of this procedure is that, because it operates outside the regime governing the conduct of arbitrations or litigation under the rules of a court, it is possible for the parties to the contract to empower the expert to reach a rapid decision. The expert panel adopts an inquisitorial role in investigating the facts and the law regarding the dispute, often with a wide discretion as to how to go about the task. The expert panel is usually required to make its decision in a matter of weeks rather than months or years. The result may be "rough justice" but it may be preferable to the uncertainties and expense that can be created by delays commonly associated with court proceedings and arbitrations.

Some infrastructure contracts provide for disputes to be referred to experts as part of the overall dispute resolution process. The experts' decisions can be binding or non-binding. If they are non-binding they can still be persuasive in encouraging the parties to settle the dispute.[101] However, unlike arbitration, expert determination does not normally have any statutory support or sanction and there are no international conventions relating to the enforcement of expert determinations.

Several changes would be required to adopt expert panels for regulatory contracts. The most obvious is that the distributor must have the unilateral right to convene the panel. If the panel can be convened only with the agreement of both parties, it is unlikely that the regulator would ever agree to convene the panel for the reasons just discussed. In addition, the regulatory contract must provide that the parties will comply with the experts' determinations.

However, a further procedure will be required, either through the local courts or through local or international arbitration, to provide an effective mechanism for enforcing the experts' decision. In some jurisdictions, the law may not support expert determination on the grounds that it illegitimately excludes or restricts the jurisdiction of the courts or that it offends against strict legal due process requirements or the principle that a person is entitled to a full trial or hearing of any matter affecting his or her civil rights and liabilities. If binding expert determination is to be adopted as the means of dispute resolution in the regulatory contract, these issues would need to be addressed in any enabling legislation.

A Specialized Appeals Tribunal

A fifth approach is a specialized appellate tribunal to adjudicate disputes between the regulator and the distribution company. A distribution company with a grievance against its regulator would *not* need to get the concurrence of the regulator in order to file a complaint with the specialized tribunal. Specialized tribunals have been created in countries as varied as England, Australia, Uganda, Tanzania and Bolivia. In Chile, a special presidential commission recommended the creation of a multi-sectoral "economic court" as a critical "second generation reform" for the country's infrastructure industries. It has also been proposed in a new national electricity law for

---

101. At the U.S. FERC, this technique is referred to as "Early Neutral Evaluation." It is defined as "an early and frank evaluation by an objective observer or 'evaluator.'" It has been used to encourage the settlement of disputes between regulated utilities and one or more of its customers. It has not been used for resolving disagreements between the regulated utility and the FERC. If a utility disagrees with a commission order, its only redress is to file an appeal in an appellate court. See *FERC ADR News*, Summer 2002, p. 1. Available at www.ferc.fed.us.

India based on the model of a specialized court that has operated successfully in the Indian telecommunications sector.[102]

What are the typical features of such tribunals? The tribunal usually hears appeals of regulators' decisions in one or more infrastructure sectors. It will usually have considerable discretion over the scope of its actions. For example, in the United Kingdom the Competition Commission, which serves as the appellate tribunal for some of the regulators, can, in some instances, supplant a regulator's decision and replace it with its own decision (Lawrence, 2002). In other countries, however, the tribunal is limited to approving or disapproving the regulator's decision.[103] The right of appeal may be granted to the company, the regulator and the company's consumers.[104] The tribunal may be a standing body (India) or simply convened on an "as needed" basis (United Kingdom) from a pre-selected group of more than 20 experts.[105] It will normally be composed of technical experts as well as lawyers. As a quasi-judicial entity, it has considerable discretion in creating its own procedures and processes. In particular, it does not have to follow the strict rules and procedures of a regular court but it does need a set of transparent and fair rules to ensure that the parties can present their cases fully. The tribunal's decisions may be appealable to the country's supreme court (India) or to international arbitration (Uganda). But if there is an appeal of the tribunal's decisions, the appeals are generally limited to narrow procedural issues rather than a complete *de novo* review of the substance of the dispute.

To date, the real-world experience with special appellate tribunals in most countries has generally been positive. Among the observed benefits are the following:

- **Special tribunals produce faster decisions.** For example, in India the Telecom Disputes Settlement and Appellate Tribunal has usually issued decisions in six to eight months as opposed to an average of three to four years for the Indian Supreme Court. However, this is not true in all countries. The UK Competition Commission seems to average about 9-12 months for some of its price reviews. But this may reflect the fact that UK commission is essentially rerunning the basic price review in some infrastructure industries rather than simply functioning as appellate review body.

---

102. See Sections 110-125 of Electricity Bill 2001 which is available on the website of the Indian Ministry of Power (http://powermin.nic.in/report/mopi_opt4.pdf). The Supreme Court of India, in a recent order overturning the decision of a state High Court, strongly recommended that future appeals of state electricity regulatory commissions be reviewed by a special national electricity tribunal rather than the state High Court. The Supreme Court wrote: "Without meaning any disrespect to the Judges of the High Court, we think neither the High Court nor the Supreme Court would in reality be appropriate appellate forums in dealing with this type of factual and technical matters." Judgement and Order of the Hon'ble Supreme Court, Re: CESC Tariff, Civil Appeal No. 4037 of 2002, October 3, 2002.

103. An appellate tribunal reviews the regulator's decisions and essentially says "yes" or "no" to the decision. If the answer is "no", then the tribunal will normally tell the regulator why it thinks that the decision was wrong on technical, legal or both grounds. In contrast, the Competition Commission in the United Kingdom has authority that goes beyond "yes" or "no" decisions. It can say "yes" or "no" or change the regulator's decision for some of the new infrastructure regulators. Because it has been given this wider authority, it is, in effect, the functional equivalent of a higher level regulator for these industries rather than just an appellate body.

104. It seems counter intuitive that the regulator would have to seek review of its own decisions. But this is effectively the case for the British electricity regulator (OFGEM) because it is not allowed to make any changes to a distribution company's existing tariff formulas unless the company agrees. If the company withholds its approval, OFGEM can mandate the tariff change only if it receives formal approval from the Competition Commission. In India, the current proposal for a national electricity appellate tribunal would also grant the right of appeal to individual electricity consumers. Given the propensity of Indian consumers to sue, the granting of this right could easily overwhelm the proposed tribunal. In contrast, distribution companies in England are required to establish a separate dispute resolution mechanism for consumer complaints and the right to go to the Competition Commission is granted only to the regulator and licensees.

105. In the United Kingdom, although the Competition Commission has no standing panels, its secretariat is a full time and permanent organization.

■ **The tribunals are likely to produce more-informed decisions.** Many of the disputes between the regulator and a distribution company will be technical or economic in nature. The judges in most regular courts, whether in developing or developed countries, generally lack the background to deal with complex technical and economic disputes. Without such knowledge, they tend to make decisions on narrow legal grounds. And even if they have the requisite technical and commercial knowledge, existing laws or legal precedents may preclude them from going beyond a review of whether the regulatory commission followed appropriate procedures. In contrast, special tribunals are specifically required to examine whether the regulator complied with substance (for example, whether the regulator implemented the tariff-setting formula) as well as process.

■ **An appellate tribunal will be familiar with the industry and may have heard similar disputes in other infrastructure industries if it has jurisdiction over several industries.** For example, some members of the UK Competition Commission have reviewed several price determinations by British regulators. In contrast, a judge in a regular court is not likely to be familiar with the technical or institutional characteristics of the industry and, if he is, there is no certainty that he will be assigned to hearing the dispute.

■ **The use of special tribunals may avoid the expense and delay inherent in international arbitration.** Special tribunals can be used for more common disputes that, if unresolved, could lead to the collapse of the regulatory contract. The existence of a special tribunal may eliminate the need to go to international dispute resolution.

■ **The use of special tribunals precludes the need to try to reform the existing court system.** Although such reforms may be desirable, it makes little sense to put reform of the power sector "on hold" pending an overhaul of the entire judicial system. As one former chairman of the U.S. Federal Energy Regulatory Commission (FERC) observed: "If you can't reform it, then just bypass it."

Partial Risk Guarantees: A Mechanism for Ensuring Commitment?

Although a dispute resolution mechanism may look fair and efficient on paper, it will be of little value if the government or regulator refuses to implement the decision produced by the court, arbitrator or a special appellate tribunal. Therefore, investors must have confidence that governments or regulators will comply with these decisions. Otherwise the regulatory contract, no matter how well designed, will have little credibility.

It has been suggested that some additional financial mechanism is needed to induce a government or regulator to honor the regulatory contract. One recent proposal is to adapt an existing World Bank financing instrument known as a "partial risk guarantee" (PRG) to provide a backstop to the regulatory system.[106] The PRG would be written to guarantee scheduled payments of principal and interest payments on debt if the private investor defaults on or delays payments because the regulator fails to honor the terms of the regulatory contract.

How Would It Work?

If a private distributor believes that the regulator or the government has not complied with the provisions of the regulatory contract, it could initiate a claim under the dispute resolution mechanism provided for in the regulatory contract. If the dispute resolution entity agrees with the distribution company, it would order the regulator to take the regulatory action (such as increase tariffs or allow the pass-through of a power-purchase cost) required by the regulatory contract.

---

106. See Gupta et al. (2002). A second possible new use for PRGs would be to guarantee the delivery of promised subsidy payment. For example, the Delhi Government recently promised that the three new private distribution companies that it would subsidize their bulk power purchases up to a ceiling of close to USD $700 million for the first five years after privatization. Such subsidies could be backed up by a guarantee.

If the regulator refuses to comply with the panel's decision, the World Bank would pay holders of the guaranteed debt for any losses in principal or interest payments that result from the failure of the regulator to comply. The World Bank would, in turn, require a counter-guarantee from the government in the form of an "indemnity agreement" that would obligate the government to reimburse the Bank for any guarantee payments that the Bank makes to lenders. In effect, the Bank would be guaranteeing a payment to holders of debt if the regulator fails to honor the outcome of the dispute resolution process.

Why Do It?

The PRG would be a form of insurance to protect against the risk that the regulator will not live up to the terms of the regulatory contract. A government official might reasonably ask: Why should the government pay for insurance to protect private investors against the consequences of the regulator's actions?

There are at least two answers to this question. First, such a guarantee is likely to generate more investor interest in purchasing the state-owned distribution enterprise. In some developing countries, it may make the difference between getting some bidders versus getting no bidders. Second, the guarantee is likely to produce higher prices for the assets that the government is selling. Investors are willing to pay more when they see less risk. They will also be willing to pay more because the PRG is likely to lower their financing costs. Past experience shows that PRGs allow investors to get debt financing when it might not otherwise be available or allows them to get lower interest rates on any debt that they acquire. So it may be in the government's self interest to "buy" this insurance if the benefits—getting serious bidders and a higher price from bidders— exceed the costs—the charge for the premium and the possible payment to the World Bank to compensate it for any payments to debt holders.[107]

The same government official might also ask a second question: Why should the government be held responsible (that is, be forced to make a guarantee payment) for the actions or decisions of an independent regulator? After all, if the regulator is truly independent, it seems contradictory to argue that the government should still held accountable for the regulator's actions.

Although this argument seems superficially plausible, it ignores the fact that the regulator is a creature of the government because government established the regulator in the first place and created the regulatory system administered by the regulator. So the government should ultimately be willing to take responsibility that the regulatory system that it created is operating as intended. Moreover, it may simply be in the government's financial interest to offer the guarantee.

Is It Feasible?

This leads us to a more difficult question: Is it realistic to expect that PRGs can be used to guarantee the performance of a multi-dimensional regulatory system? To date, PRGs have never been used for this purpose, though they have been used in other contexts. For example, the World Bank has issued PRGs to support several privately financed IPPs projects.[108] In these instances, the Bank issued PRGs to guarantee that a government-owned buyer would make payments for power purchased under the terms of power purchase agreement signed with a private developer. In these cases, the trigger for payments under the PRG was relatively straightforward: either the government-owned buyer made payments for the electricity supplied or it did not.

---

107. A government could determine these costs and benefits by seeking bids with and without the guarantees to see the effect of the guarantees on offer prices.

108. See World Bank (April 2002). PRGs have also been used by MIGA to insure against other forms of political risk such as changes in laws, outbreak of war, breach and repudiation of contracts, expropriation and access to currency convertibility. Information on guarantees is available at www.miga.org and www.worldbank.org/guarantees. For an overview of both World Bank and non-World Bank guarantee instruments, see Bubnova (1999).

Guaranteeing the performance of a multi-faceted regulatory system is clearly more complicated because regulatory systems are defined by both substance and process. For example, a regulator may decide not to allow a distribution company to raise tariffs to pay for additional investments, even though the terms of the multi-year tariff formula provide for an increase when such investments are made. Rather than directly and openly violate the terms of the tariff formula, the regulator might argue that it cannot raise tariffs because the distribution company did not provide adequate and timely information to allow it to determine if the investments were prudent or fell within a pre-approved category. In this situation, the regulator may be hiding behind regulatory processes to avoid raising tariffs. Unless the regulatory contract is clear on both process (such as maximum time before the regulator must make a decision and information that must be provided) and substance (such as the tariff increase that results from a given level of investments), it will be difficult for an arbitrator or specialized court to determine whether the contract has been violated.

The PRG will be difficult to enforce if the regulatory contract is vague. This is a problem in the tariff sections of several of the concession agreements for private distribution companies in Brazil. For example, in describing how the regulator will reset tariffs at the end of the first multi-year tariff period, the only guidance, as discussed earlier, is a single sentence that states that the Brazilian regulator

> shall process the revision of the amounts of rates for commercialization of power, altering them upwards or downwards, taking into account the cost and market structures of the concessionaire, the levels of rates practiced by similar companies in the nationwide and international context, and stimuli for efficiency and for reasonableness of rates.[109]

The vagueness of this sentence has led to major battles in Brazil over its interpretation as the first tariff period is coming to a close for more than 50 Brazilian distribution companies.[110] The obvious lesson from the Brazilian experience is that the viability of a creating a PRG for a regulatory system will depend critically on the specificity of the language in the underlying regulatory contract.

---

109. Concession Agreement for AES Sul, Article 7, Sub-Article 6, November 6, 1997.

110. For example, ANEEL and the distribution companies have a major disagreement over the allowed capital base that will be used to determine allowed revenues in future multi-year tariff periods. ANEEL has proposed a methodology which the distribution companies argue would produce a regulatory capital base of US$4 billion for 16 of the largest distribution companies, while the companies contend that they are entitled to a regulatory capital base of about US$17 billion. Although there are also disputes over asset valuation in other Latin American countries such as Chile and Peru, the disputes are over the details of implementing a particular asset valuation methodology rather than the threshold issue of which of several methodologies should be used.

CHAPTER 7

CONCLUDING OBSERVATIONS

"Investors need confidence. Consumers need protection."

—Speaker at a conference on private participation
in Chinese infrastructure, November 2001

The key lessons learned from the experience of developing and developed countries with regulation by contract are as follows:

1. Independence is not enough.
2. The regulatory contract must be a political contract.
3. Regulation by contract versus regulation by commission is a false dichotomy.
4. Regulation by contract is a new name for an old paradigm.
5. Electricity consumers cannot be the forgotten third party to a regulatory contract.
6. Investors must have confidence that the contract will be enforced fairly and efficiently.
7. The heart of a regulatory contract is a pre-specified, performance based, multi-year tariff-setting system.
8. A regulatory contract is sustainable only if the underlying economics are viable.
9. A multi-year tariff system can be put into operation even in the absence of high-quality data.
10. Regulation by contract should be reserved for private distribution companies.

1. Independence is not Enough.

- Over the last decade, regulatory "independence" has been a key element of the recipe for successful power sector reform recommended by the World Bank and other development organizations. The rationale for the recommendation was the belief that reform would fail (especially if it involved privatization) unless tariff setting is depoliticized. It was thought that an independent regulator—a regulator that is free to make decisions on tariffs and other regulatory matters without first obtaining the approval of political authorities—would do a better job of setting cost-recovering tariffs than a government ministry facing day-to-day political pressures.

- Now, with the benefit of more than ten years of experience, it is clear that independence is not enough. The reality in many countries is that independence has never been achieved. Regulatory independence has been more theoretical than real. Despite the many safeguards that exist in new laws, it has been difficult to protect new commissions from direct or indirect political pressures to avoid actions that a government thinks will be politically damaging. Most new regulators in developing countries, when asked whether they have the independence provided for in law, will either say "no" or avert their glance and change the subject.

- Even in those countries where effective independent regulatory decision-making has been achieved, commissions are not likely to follow policies that balance consumer and private investor interests because:

  - **Starting conditions are bad.** The typical starting conditions for a regulator in a developing country are that: tariffs do not cover costs; some customers (usually industrial users) heavily subsidize the consumption of other customers (usually residential users); interruptions are frequent; electricity is widely stolen by rich and poor customers (frequently with the active support of existing employees); and many rural citizens lack access to electricity. Given these starting conditions, it is unrealistic to expect that an independent regulatory commission will be able to close the gap between revenues and costs and rebalance tariffs across classes under the guise of simply making some technical tariff adjustments. The reality is that the government that created the commission has been running away or hiding from both problems for many years.

  - **Transitions take longer than expected.** Consumers expect much more of private companies than state-owned enterprises. Consumers understandably lose patience if tariffs go up immediately but service improvements lag behind. When this happens, the regulators get blamed. Therefore, it is not surprising that most regulators, when faced with this situation, will try to find a way not to raise tariffs, especially if their legal mandate consists of nothing more than principles, goals and objectives (soft law).

  - **The regulator cannot do it alone.** It is relatively easy to pass a reform law but the commercial viability of a distribution company depends on the government paying its electricity bills, providing basic law and order so that the company can collect from non-paying customers and, in some cases, providing subsidies for a transition period. If the government is unwilling or unable to take these actions, there is little that a regulator can do to create an economically viable enterprise. The fact that the regulator is independent is largely irrelevant.

  - **Foreign ownership is often viewed as a new form of colonialism.** If tariffs are not raised prior to privatization, they will have to be raised soon after privatization. Most electricity consumers in countries that are former colonies will view this as exploitation unless there is an obvious and significant improvement in quality of service. The situation is especially sensitive if the new owner is a foreign company.

▪ **The overall experience of the past decade suggests that independence is not enough.** Independence must also be combined with an explicit and binding regulatory contract established prior to privatization. For most developing countries, the Anglo-American tradition of regulatory independence must be combined with the French tradition of detailed regulatory contracts. In other words, the single most important lesson of the last ten years is that independence must be "backstopped" by a regulatory agreement that goes beyond general principles. And the key element of the regulatory contract should be a well-specified, multi-year tariff-setting system that is required by law and specified in concessions, licenses and other regulatory instruments (hard law).

2. The Regulatory Contract Must be a Political Contract.

▪ A regulatory contract must inevitably be a political contract between the government and the new private owner of the distribution enterprise because the commitment will not be believable unless it is an explicit commitment of the country's highest political authorities. It is naïve to believe that the design of the regulatory contract can or even should be depoliticized.

▪ However, even though the regulatory contract should be a political contract, the political authorities that created the contract need not also be responsible for implementing it on a day-to-day basis. Once the regulatory contract is in place (i.e., the political deal has been made), the contract is best administered by an independent regulator. This makes it difficult for the government to change its mind after it agrees to the contract. The temptation for a government to renege on a regulatory contract, either openly or in hidden ways, will be very high if the transition is not smooth (and transitions, almost by definition, are never smooth). Also, it is unrealistic to expect that a future government, especially if it is from the opposition party, will be equally committed to honoring the regulatory contract. So it is best to create a regulatory contract so that a new government can credibly say: "It is beyond my control."

▪ A law is the highest expression of a country's political commitment. Therefore, the underlying principles and initial parameters of the regulatory contract should be clearly specified in the country's primary or secondary electricity laws (Chile, Argentina, Bolivia and Peru). A regulatory contract is less likely to survive if it is poorly specified (Brazil) or exists only within a stand-alone concession or license agreement with little clear support in national laws (Brazil).

▪ A regulatory contract will not be credible if international investors believe that its multi-year, tariff-setting provisions are vulnerable to legal challenge because such a tariff-setting system was not anticipated when the law was written (as is the case in India). The regulatory contract will also not be credible unless the government is empowered to design the contract and the regulator is empowered to enforce it. These are unnecessary legal risks that usually can be eliminated by amending existing laws.

▪ The regulatory contract will just be "pretty poetry" unless the government also takes actions to support the contract. The single best test of a government's ongoing political commitment is the day-to-day support that it provides to the distribution company to reduce theft. A government can publicly demonstrate its commitment to "law and order" through the passage and enforcement of anti-theft legislation that allows for disconnection and prosecution of those who steal electricity. However, the commitment requires more than just passing a law. A good sign of serious political commitment is if the government successfully prosecutes one or two rich or politically well-connected individuals that have been stealing electricity. Another sign is if the government pays its own electricity bills. If a government is unwilling to take such steps, there is little point in trying to create a regulatory contract.

3. "Regulation by Contract Versus Regulation by Commission" is a False Dichotomy.

- The real choice is between an independent regulator with substantial discretion and an independent regulator with little discretion, especially in the first post-privatization tariff period.
- An independent regulator with substantial discretion is one who sets prices under general, broadly worded tariff-setting principles (India). This is also the U.S. system, where the tariff guidance in the law is often limited to a general statement that tariffs must be "just and reasonable and not unduly discriminatory." This system has worked well in the United States because of 70 years of legal precedents as to what the principles mean in application combined with an independent judiciary to ensure that the precedents are not ignored. When this regulatory system is transplanted to a developing country, it usually will not work for several reasons: there are no legal precedents (or the precedents may have little or no legal significance if it is a civil law country); the country's judiciary is neither independent or knowledgeable; and the starting conditions are so bad that that the regulator will not be able to withstand the open or hidden pressure to keep tariffs low through a variety of techniques (for example, process delays, setting allowed revenues based on impossible to achieve efficiency targets). If the regulatory system in a developing country consists of an independent regulator who operates under broadly worded tariff principles, foreign investors will not invest.
- The better alternative is to create an independent regulator who sets prices under a well-specified, pre-determined, multi-year tariff-setting system (Bolivia, Chile and Peru). "Well-defined" and "pre-determined" mean that specific tariff formulas and target parameters are established as part of the privatization process. In order to reduce the risk of revenue uncertainty to a manageable level for investors, the regulator must have little discretion on both substance and process during the initial post-privatization, tariff-setting period. In this critical first tariff period, the regulator needs to act more as a "referee" than as a "judge." The regulator's role in the first period should be limited to making certain that the tariff formula in the regulator contract is correctly applied and that true-ups and pre-scheduled tariff adjustments are processed in timely way.
- Transparency works. Even if a regulator's legal authority is limited to making recommendations to a minister, the minister will find it difficult to overturn the regulator's recommendations if they are made publicly and are backed up with a clear technical analysis.

4. Regulation by Contract is a New Name for an Old Paradigm.

- Regulation by contract—an independent or quasi-independent regulator administering a well-specified tariff-setting system that is embedded in laws, concessions and regulations—has been the norm for distribution privatizations throughout Latin America for more than 15 years.
- Regulation by contract is more difficult for distribution than generation because the distribution business has many more strands to it that affect the quality of service to thousands of customers and the need for substantial ongoing investments. Even so, such contracts have been written and honored in several Latin American countries for more than a decade.
- Process is important. The single most common mistake in writing regulatory contracts is to focus on the tariff-setting principles and formulas while ignoring the regulatory processes needed to implement the principles and formulas. With the exception of Brazil, the Latin American regulatory contracts for distribution have generally succeeded because they have specified principles, formulas and processes.

- Regulation by contract will not survive a major macro-economic "meltdown" (Argentina), but neither would any other regulatory system.
- It is not feasible to write a regulatory contract for all regulatory decisions. For example, if the government decides to unbundle the sector (that is, create separate generation, transmission and distribution entities), this will inevitably lead to the creation of a centralized or decentralized bulk power market. If the regulator is charged with monitoring the market, he or she will need considerable discretion in deciding the information that is needed and the actions that should be taken if market participants are found to have market power. Therefore, a single regulator may need considerable discretion for some decisions and little discretion for others.

5. Electricity Consumers Cannot be the Forgotten Third Party to a Regulatory Contract.

- Although the government or the regulator signs the regulatory contract, it must not forget that it is acting as an agent for consumers.
- The government and regulator must be able to persuade consumers that the initial contract is fair and that it will be fairly enforced.
- If the contract leads to higher prices, consumers must see improvements in service sooner rather than later.
- If consumers fail to see any obvious benefits from the regulatory contract ("early wins"), it will be politically unsustainable.
- Consumers are often willing to pay substantially more for reliable electricity because they recognize that cheap electricity that does not arrive has no value.
- The key task for the government and the regulator is to ensure that there is a fair balance between the interests of the consumer and the interests of the investor. This involves attracting the investment that the consumer needs but at the same time minimizing the need for new investment by using existing resources more efficiently.

6. Investors Must have Confidence that the Contract will be Enforced Fairly and Efficiently.

- Contract disputes are inevitable because no regulatory contract can envisage all eventualities.
- In most developing countries, the existing court system is not a viable dispute resolution mechanism for disputes between the regulator and the company. Existing courts are slow, not likely to have the expertise to deal with complicated technical and economic disputes, and may be corrupt.
- International arbitration of regulatory disputes under international rules will make a proposed distribution privatization much more appealing to international investors. However, international arbitration is usually expensive and cumbersome. If it is invoked, it usually means that the regulatory contract is dangerously close to complete collapse. It is preferable to combine the "backstop" of international arbitration with less costly forms of dispute resolution that can prevent one or more smaller disputes from exploding into a big dispute.
- Some countries have had success in creating standing expert panels that can be used not only to adjudicate disputes through formal arbitration but also to give a preliminary view or report on the facts of the dispute as presented to them. These findings of fact, because they are made by a panel or well-respected and experienced individuals, can be prepared quickly and are a powerful tool for the parties to use to settle the dispute. If such a panel

is created, it effectively performs two functions: first, as an expert fact-finding panel and second, as an arbitration panel.

■ An expert panel will not be viable if it can be convened only with the agreement of the regulator (Brazil). It is unrealistic to expect that the regulator would voluntarily agree to agree such a panel because it is tantamount to admission by the regulator that his decision may have been flawed. If an expert panel is to be used, the licensee must have the legal right to require that it be convened.

■ Mediation may be a viable mechanism for disputes involving the regulated company and its customers. It may also be workable for designing new rules. However, it is not likely to be a viable mechanism for disputes between a distribution company and the regulator once the regulator has issued a formal decision. In such circumstances, the regulator will have little or no incentive to enter into mediation. Nor does it make sense to mandate that the regulator enter into mediation when requested by the company. Although it may be possible to force the regulator to sit in a mediation room, it will be a wasted effort because the regulator will still have no incentive to negotiate in good faith.

■ Another approach, adopted in several developing and developed countries, is to give the distribution company the right to appeal the regulator's decisions to a specialized appellate tribunal that reviews decisions of one or all infrastructure regulators. The tribunal should be explicitly authorized to examine the substantive as well as the legal aspects of the dispute.

■ The World Bank should explore the feasibility of backstopping regulatory contracts by guaranteeing that the outcome of the dispute resolution mechanism will be honored.

7. The Heart of a Regulatory Contract is a Pre-Specified, Performance-Based, Multi-Year Tariff-Setting System.

■ The multi-year tariff system should include benchmarks or targets for controllable costs and automatic pass-through for non-controllable costs. The categorization of costs may change over time as industry structure changes. However, the regulator should be allowed to change the tariff treatment of a particular cost only at the end of a multi-year tariff period.

■ The benchmarks for controllable costs can be based on the company's historic performance, an external index or the performance of comparable companies. The benchmarks must be credible and set achievable targets or they will be ineffective as incentives to change behavior. In establishing a benchmark, the tariff formula should distinguish whether price, quantity or both elements are under the control of the company.

■ Benchmarks or targets should be combined with incentive mechanisms. Such incentive mechanisms should be limited to costs or operating parameters that are measurable, material, controllable and predictable. At any one time, there should be no more than 3 or 4 incentive mechanisms in operation.

■ The two most important benchmarks in many developing and former socialist countries are the technical and commercial loss-reduction targets and the price paid for discretionary power purchases. The financial viability of a new private distribution entity will depend critically on its ability to reduce commercial losses (theft).

■ Benchmarks should be used for establishing a maximum pass-through price for power purchases. A well-designed benchmark for power purchases should possess three characteristics. First, it should not be set too low. If the benchmark is too low (Chile and Brazil), generators will be unwilling to sign contracts with distributors for new capacity and this will eventually lead to shortages. If feasible, the benchmark should be based on market measures (Colombia and the Netherlands) rather than administrative projections of supply costs (Brazil and California). Second, any market benchmark should not be based solely on the price of spot energy (Argentina). It must be defined more broadly so that a distribution company will have incentives to make short, intermediate and long purchases that allow it to hedge for the risk of future price fluctuations (Colombia and the Netherlands). Third, distributors must have reasonable opportunity to make profits on purchases so that they will have an incentive to purchase efficiently.

- Pass-through of non-controllable costs should be done frequently and automatically. The tariff-setting system must also include a mechanism for the pass-through of costs associated with unanticipated external events such as natural disasters or major changes in law, regulations and some taxes. Whenever possible, the regulatory contract should include specific "trigger" mechanisms to adjust tariffs for extraordinary events. In developing countries, the civil law concept of restoring the enterprise's "financial-economic equilibrium" is not a workable approach for dealing with extraordinary events.
- The tariff-setting system must also pay particular attention to the regulatory review of new investments. A regulatory system that requires an investment-by-investment review, either on an ex ante or ex post basis, is not workable. The better approach is to set quality-of-service standards (performance regulation) rather than engaging in regulatory reviews of individual investments (conduct regulation).
- Any tariff-setting system should explicitly assign risk to the company, its customers or the government. Private investors should only be assigned risks that they can control or mitigate. Private investors must be allowed to recover the costs of any risks that they bear for their customers. The allocation of risk will need to vary depending on starting conditions. The worse the starting conditions, the greater the risk that must remain with government or consumers.
- The regulatory contract cannot be limited to a single multi-year tariff period following privatization. At a minimum, the actual formulas should be specified for the first period and the principles and general methodologies should be specified for subsequent tariff periods.
- In countries with more than one distribution company, the regulator should require the companies to provide comparable data on costs and operating performance that can be used to establish benchmarks.

8. A Regulatory Contract is Sustainable Only If the Underlying Economics are Viable.

- Regulation by contract is not a "magic bullet." It will not work if there is a large gap between costs and revenues.
- The gap must be closed by lowering costs (for example, reducing technical and commercial losses that lead to unnecessary power purchases), increasing revenues (for example, metering and billing farmers in India for the power that they consume), or both.
- International and domestic investors will incur some costs in hard currencies. Even if the domestic tariffs are initially high enough to cover these non-domestic costs, this can quickly change if the local currency loses value relative to hard currencies. Therefore, investors must receive some protection (usually indexing) against depreciation of the domestic currency. Indexing should be limited to costs that will be incurred in foreign currencies (usually about 40 to 60 percent of the retail tariff) rather than indexing of a full 100 percent of the tariff (as was the case in Argentina). However, any indexing system, no matter how well designed, will not be politically sustainable if the local currency experiences a major loss in value.
- In some developing countries, the regulatory contract will need to be combined with transition-period subsidies to the private company, its customers or both. The easiest way

to deliver a subsidy to a distribution company is by subsidizing the cost of the power that it purchases from government suppliers or private suppliers.

■ A government should always require a *quid pro quo* for any subsidies that it funds. For example, a government may decide to subsidize the cost of connecting new rural customers and the bills of poor customers throughout the system. To receive these subsidies, the company must show that its connections of new customers meet pre-specified technical standards and the customer must show that it paid the unsubsidized portion of his bill.

■ When the revenue-cost gap is large, the principal purpose of the subsidies is to prevent rate shock rather than to subsidize the private company.

■ The World Bank should consider giving loans for transition period subsidies combined with guarantee mechanisms to ensure that the subsidies are actually delivered to the intended recipients.

9. A Multi-Year Tariff System Can be Put into Operation Even in the Absence of High-Quality Data.

■ The existing quality of cost and technical information is usually poor for state-owned enterprises in developing and former socialist countries.

■ The introduction of performance-based multi-year tariffs should not be delayed until the data "get better."

■ Data quality will improve through privatization, especially if better data can be specified as a performance element in the regulatory contract.

■ If there is a political concern that investors will be able to earn high profits because of poor data quality, then the tariff system should include a within–tariff-period "sharing" mechanism between the distribution companies and its customers. Revenue-sharing mechanisms are easier to implement and less vulnerable to "gaming" than profit sharing mechanisms.

10. Regulation by Contract Should be Reserved for Private Distribution Companies.

■ In developing countries, regulation by contract rarely works for state-owned power enterprises. This is because most state-owned enterprises do not respond to normal commercial incentives.

■ Thus there is little to be gained in creating a new independent regulator to regulate a state-owned power enterprise. Despite the fact that the new regulator may have all the paraphernalia and trappings of an independent regulatory system, it will accomplish little or nothing. Or in the words of one new regulator who was forced to regulate an existing state-owned enterprise: "I write longer and longer orders but less and less happens."

■ For most state-owned power enterprises, institutional change changes nothing.

CONTROLLABLE AND NON-CONTROLLABLE COSTS: A PROPOSED REGULATORY FRAMEWORK

Note: Authors' comments are in italics.

(1) A multi-year tariff-setting formula may distinguish between the treatment of input costs based on different degrees of effective control—that is, the ability of a distribution and retail supply licensee to significantly influence the cost and quality such that:

  (a) The prescribed tariff treatment may differ depending on the degree of effective control exercised by the Licensee over the price and/or quantity of a particular input. [*Suppose that a distribution company is assigned vesting contracts for some or all of its supply needs as part of the privatization package. As a consequence, it will have no control over the price paid for this power over the life of the contract. However, it may have control over the overall quantity of power purchased depending on its success in reducing technical and commercial losses on its distribution systems. For any new purchases, the distribution company will generally have control over both price and quantity.*]

  (b) Automatic cost pass-through should be limited to changes in components of an input cost (i.e., price, quantity or both) that are beyond the control of the Licensee, on a pre-determined periodicity. For any delay in implementing such automatic cost pass-through beyond 90 days, the Licensee shall be compensated by allowing interest on the additional capital/working capital for the period of delay. This interest shall be reflected in the Licensee's tariff as an automatic pass-through.

  (c) A Licensee's degree of effective control over an input cost may change over time. The Commission has the authority to change the tariff treatment of an input cost in the tariff order issued for a new multi-year tariff period but not during a multi-year tariff period. If the Commission changes the tariff treatment for a particular input cost, it must provide reasons in writing for the change.

(2) The Commission shall utilize, whenever feasible, pre-determined indices and external benchmarks for costs under the control of the Licensee.

(3) The Commission shall establish incentive mechanisms that provide Licensees with rewards and/or penalties based on their performance relating to benchmarks established for particular cost and/or operational targets. [*In developed countries, the key benchmark is usually an overall efficiency factor while in developing countries it is likely to be commercial and technical loss reduction and sometimes new customer connections.*]

(4) The design and implementation of the tariff treatment of both controllable costs and non-controllable costs should be guided by the overriding principles of implementability and reliable verification.

(5) The division between controllable and non-controllable costs in a multi-year tariff formula will produce an allocation of risk between different stakeholders like the State Government, the Licensee, and the Consumers. In determining a fair and efficient allocation of risk, the State Government and Commission should be guided by the following general principles:

    (a) A risk should be borne by the entity best able to control or mitigate the risk.

    (b) In determining the appropriate expected rate of return for a Licensee, the Commission shall ensure that the risk being borne by the Licensee is duly taken into account.

(6) If an unforeseen extraneous event occurs that has a material adverse impact on controllable costs, a Licensee may seek changes in the tariff to offset the material adverse impact of this event.

(7) For claiming adjustment because of an adverse material impact of an unforeseen extraordinary event, a licensee may file an application to the Commission seeking tariff changes to offset the material adverse impact. The application shall be accompanied by evidence and calculations to demonstrate that the event was extraordinary and uncontrollable, and the extent of the material adverse impact on the Licensee's costs and revenue. Such events may include, but not be limited to, damage caused by acts of God, a calculation of and changes in taxes, duties, and environmental regulations.

(8) Where an extraordinary event has produced a positive material impact on the Licensee, the Commission may undertake a study to determine whether a material positive impact has occurred. If a material positive impact has occurred the Commission may propose a suitable tariff change, with the burden of proof for demonstrating the uncontrollable nature of the event and its effect on the Licensee's cost and revenues falling on the Commission. Any Licensee investigated for an extraordinary material positive impact must cooperate with the Commission and provide whatever information is requested in a timely manner.

(9) If the Commission considers that the proposed tariff reconciliation or amendment under sub-sections (7) or (8) of a licensee is not permissible it shall, within 60 days (or such other period as may be prescribed by the Commission) of receipt of all the information which it required, and after consultation with the Commission Advisory Committee and the licensee, notify the licensee that

    (a) the reconciliation or the unforeseen adjustment sought is not permissible, or

    (b) in case the Commission is convinced that an adjustment (either positive or negative) is justified but the proposed magnitude of the adjustment is not justified, it shall specify an alternative adjustment that must be adopted by the Licensee.

(10) If the Commission determines that a material adverse impact has been suffered by the licensee arising due to an extraordinary unforeseen event which warrants a tariff adjustment, it shall determine the tariff adjustment taking into account

    (a) the time period (the 'recovery' period) over which the incremental costs should be recovered (capped at the remaining life of the current multi-year tariff period plus an additional multi-year tariff period); and

    (b) the incremental price increase required to ensure that the company is no worse-off financially than originally planned if this event had not occurred.

If the recovery period extends into the next multi-year tariff period, the additional price increase should be treated as a ring-fenced revenue stream regulated and should be treated as an automatic pass-through cost.

OBLIGATION TO SERVE: A PROPOSED REGULATORY FRAMEWORK

Note: Authors' comments are in italics.

(1) The Licensees are obliged to supply consumers within the pre-defined area of service of a radius of up to 400 meters around existing distribution facilities owned or leased by the Licensee unless certain distribution facilities and the customers served by these facilities are specifically excluded from a Licensee's area of service. *Distribution facilities* means distribution substations and lines that are used for the provision of distribution service to customers under the conditions included in the License. [*This is the approach used in most privatizations of distribution in Latin America. It uses a "facilities-based" approach to defining service area. An alternative approach would be to impose an obligation to serve anyone within a defined geographic area such as a state or a district. This second, more open-ended obligation is riskier for a distribution company if the defined area is rural and includes many non-connected households.*]

(2) The specific radius for different distribution facilities and regions shall be established by the Government for the Transition Arrangement [*In this country, the government rather than the regulator will specify the tariff-setting system in the first multi-year, post-privatization tariff period. This reflects a policy decision that the government is more likely to be sensitive to the tariff conditions that will support a sustainable privatization than the regulator.*] and by the Commission thereafter. The radius may vary within a licensee's area of service.

(3) Once the initial bands for area of service are established by the Government, they cannot be changed through an increase or a decrease unless the Licensee agrees to the modifications.

(4) Within this area of service, Licensees are required to satisfy the Quality-of-Service Standards based upon Schedule X principles *See Appendix C*—by the Government at the

beginning of the transition period, or by the Commission in subsequent multi-year tariff periods.

(5) Subject to any Transition Arrangement stipulated under Section X, the Commission shall establish and/or revise a schedule of charges and procedures applicable to connections for different types of new customers, transfer of ownership of existing connections, reconnection of customers and customer-requested changes in service categories for existing customers within the area of service defined in clauses 1 and 2 above. The schedule of charges may allow for customer contributions to the cost of connections.

(6) The Government shall be entitled to make "subsidy policy decisions" for providing such connections.

(7) Subject to a decision of the State Government or the Commission to introduce competition in retail supply, [*The law would be improved if it included conditions that the Government or Commission must satisfy before introducing retail competition. For example, should existing licensees be compensated for stranded costs?*] the Licensee shall have the exclusive right to provide a bundled Distribution and Retail Supply within its specified area of service or an exclusive right to provide unbundled Distribution service or a combination of the two services as may be specified in its License. The obligation to provide a bundled Distribution and Retail Supply or an unbundled Distribution service extends to every person living within the area of service (i) who requests the service, and (ii) who agrees to comply with the procedures and pays the charges for the connection based on the schedule approved by the Commission. [*This paragraph reflects a policy decision to delay the introduction of retail competition. This reflects the view that it would be costly and complicated to introduce retail competition at the time of privatization. In Latin America, retail competition is being phased in— that is, the right to choose is initially given just to larger customers.*]

(8) A Licensee may delegate its obligation to provide bundled Distribution and Retail Supply services within its area of service to other entities provided that:

   (a) The Licensee enters into a binding arrangement with such delegatee to secure Distribution and Retail Supply of electricity to the area, and

   (b) The Licensee continues to be responsible for the Distribution and Retail Supply of electricity therein.

(9) Beyond its specified area of service, the Licensee is not obligated to extend bundled Distribution and Retail Supply service or unbundled Distribution service to new customers. However,

   (a) A licensee may approach the Commission to seek approval for expansion of its area of service by filing an appropriate application.

   (b) The Commission and the Government shall encourage expansion of the coverage to areas that are not under supply.

   (c) The Commission shall pass appropriate orders allowing or refusing to permit the licensee to expand its area of service based on terms and conditions deemed appropriate within [45 days] of receipt of application under Clause (a) above. In the event that no order is communicated by the Commission to the licensee within said 45 days on its application, the permission shall be deemed to have been granted.

   (d) If the Commission approves the expansion of the Licensee's facilities to provide bundled Distribution and Retail Supply service or unbundled Distribution service to additional customers, the Licensee's specified area of service shall be redefined to cover the new customers.

   (e) The Commission may grant an expansion of the Licensee's area of service on either an exclusive or non-exclusive basis.
      [*This allows for other entities to compete for the right to supply unserved areas. There is no presumption that the Licensee will have a superior right to serve new customers outside its original service area.*]

(10) The Government may define and implement schemes/programs intended to extend service to new areas not in the Licensee's area of service, including provision of subsidy funds required for that purpose. Such schemes/programs shall clearly define conditions for participation of existing Licensees, new Licensees and others in extension of such services and for participation in subsidy schemes/programs. [*The reference to "others" implies that such entities do not necessarily require licenses. It would be over-regulation to require, for example, that a small mini-grid operator must satisfy all the terms and conditions contained in a regular Distribution and Retail Supply License.*]

QUALITY OF SERVICE: A PROPOSED REGULATORY FRAMEWORK

A ll customers of the Distribution Licensees are entitled to an economic and reliable supply of electricity commensurate with the prices that they pay for electricity. Quality-of-service standards should be established to ensure that the licensee does not have an incentive to lower costs by lowering quality below the levels sought by their customers. Therefore, the Commission, or the Government for the transition period described in Section X, shall specify quality-of-service standards that satisfy the following principles.

a. Quality-of-service standards should be established for those dimensions of service that are important to consumers, controllable by the licensee and capable of being measured on a reasonably objective basis.

b. Quality-of-service standards may be established for technical and commercial dimensions of service. Technical standards may include, but not be limited to, attributes such as frequency of outages, duration of outages, stability of voltage and frequency relative to targeted levels. Commercial standards may include, but not be limited to, connection time for new customers, accuracy in meter reading and billing and response time to customer complaints. Any required standards must be capable of being measured in a cost-efficient manner and amenable to auditing. The licensee must publicize the standards to customers.

c. Quality-of-service standards need not be uniform across all customer categories or geographic areas. The standards should be based on customers' preferences and their willingness to pay for the costs of providing the specified level of quality as determined by the Commission, except for the transition period specified in Section X when the standards may be established by the Government.

d. Quality-of-service standards and associated penalties and rewards may be phased-in over time. However, standards may not be changed during a multi-year tariff period unless the changes were pre-specified at the beginning of the tariff period or are agreed to by the licensee. The standards may be based on the licensee's own past performance or the performance of other comparable licensees in the country and elsewhere in the world. The standards may be specified as guaranteed standards where the standard must be achieved in all specified cases and overall standards where the standard must be achieved on average across a specified customer category but need not be satisfied for all customers in the category.

e. After a phase-in period, sanctions or penalties may be imposed for failure to meet pre-specified quality-of-service standards. Any penalties should be related to estimates of the disutility experienced by the customer (based, where feasible, on estimates of the cost to the customer of not being served) and the costs likely to be incurred by the licensee in meeting the standards. Rewards may be granted to Distribution Licensees that meet targets associated with one or more pre-specified quality-of-service standards. Any system of rewards and penalties must be efficient, equitable and likely to enhance customer welfare. The magnitude of the rewards and penalties need not be the same across customer categories or geographic areas.

f. Penalties may be paid to individual consumers or to a general fund, administered by the Commission, that can used to provide subsidies to economically disadvantaged customers. Penalties cannot be used to support the budget of the Commission or any other governmental entity.

g. The total amount of revenues earned from rewards or lost from penalties should be capped at no more than 4 percent of estimated total revenues earned from electricity sales to retail customers.

h. Any changes in the quality-of-service standards should be synchronized with the regulatory proceeding to update the tariffs for a new multi-year period. In this proceeding, the Commission will appoint an independent and qualified consultant to produce estimates of the cost of not supplying energy to the principal categories of customers. The results of this study should be made available to the general public for their comments before the Commission issues revised quality-of-service standards and associated rewards and penalties for the subsequent multi-year period.

i. Although the Commission has the ultimate authority to adjudicate disputes between a licensee and its customers over compliance with pre-specified quality-of-service standards, the Commission has the authority to delegate this function to other entities. If the Commission chooses to delegate some or all of this function to another entity, the Commission still has the obligation to monitor the effectiveness and efficiency of the alternative complaint handling system.

j. The Commission shall establish a reliable, objective and publicly available monitoring system that compares the quality-of-service provided by Distribution Licensees. The focus of the monitoring system should be on the performance of the Licensee with respect to the standards rather than on the expenditures made by the Licensee to try to achieve the standards. The monitoring system can be based on statistically valid samples rather than full coverage to reduce the cost of creating and maintaining the system. The Commission has the authority to require licensees to provide the information necessary to create and operate such a system provided that the licensees are allowed to recover these costs in their tariffs. The Commission may require independent verification of the information provided by licensees to ensure that it is accurate and valid.

REFERENCES

Araujo, Joao Lizardo R. Hermes de. 2001. "Investment in the Brazilian ESI: What Went Wrong? What Should Be Done?" Universidade Federal do Rio de Janeiro, Brazil.

Alexander, Ian. 2001. "Financial Techniques: Accounting Approaches and Asset Valuation." Power Point Presentation at SAFIR Core Course, October 11, Agra, India. Available at www.ppiaf.org/toolkits/safir/agenda11.htm.

Alexander, Ian and Clive Harris. 2001. "Incentive Regulation and Multi-year Price Controls: An Application to Regulation of Power Distribution in India." *International Journal of Regulation and Governance*, Volume 1:1-22.

Alexander, Ian and Chris Shugart. 1999. "Risk, Volatility and Smoothing: Regulatory Options for Controlling Prices." World Bank and European Bank for Reconstruction and Development, unpublished paper, November.

Andhra Pradesh Electricity Regulatory Commission. 2002a. "Long Term Tariff Setting Principles." Available at www.ercap.org/tariff/LongTermTariffPrinciples.htm.

———. 2002b. Order No. 527, "On the Application of APTRANSCO for the consent of the PPA with Andhra Power Ltd (BAPL)." December 13. Available at www.ercap.org/ppp/ppp.htm.

Besant-Jones, John and Bernard Tenenbaum. 2001. "Lessons from California's Power Crisis." *Finance and Development* (September), 24-28. Available at www.worldbank.org/html/fpd/energy/calexp.html.

Baldwin, Robert and Martin Cave. 1999. *Understanding Regulation: Theory, Strategy and Practice*. Oxford University Press.

Baumol, William J., Paul L. Joskow, and Alfred Kahn. 1996. *The Challenge for Federal and State Regulators: Transition from Regulation to Efficient Competition in Electric Power*. Edison Electric Institute.

Block, Corinne. 1998. *Delegated Management: A Solution for the South African Electricity Sector*. Association of Municipal Technical Electric Utilities.

Brown, Ashley C. and Ericson De Paula. 2002. *Strengthening the Institutional and Regulatory Structure of the Brazilian Power Sector.* Report prepared for the Brazilian Ministry of Mines and Energy by the Public-Private Infrastructure Advisory Facility. Available at http://rru.worldbank.org/energy.

Bubnova, Nina. 1999. "Guarantees and Insurance for Re-Allocation and Mitigating Political and Regulatory Risks in Infrastructure Investment: Market Analysis." Available at www.worldbank.org/riskconference/papers_txt.htm.

Carne, Simon, et al. 1999. *The Competition and Policy Implications of Regulatory Depreciation and the Regulatory Asset Base.* London Business School, *Regulation Initiative Discussion Paper Series*, Number 25, London.

Costello, Ken. 2002. "Regulatory Questions on Hedging: The Case of Natural Gas." *The Electricity Journal* (May), 43-51.

Demsetz, Harold. 1968. "Why Regulate Utilities?" *Journal of Law and Economics*, Volume 11, April.

DTE. 2000. *Guidelines for price cap regulation of the Dutch electricity sector for the period from 2000 to 2003.* Available at www.nma-dte.nl/en/default.htm.

Fernando, C.S. and P.R. Kleindoerfer. 1997. "Integrating Financial and Physical Contracting in Electric Power Markets." In *The Virtual Utility*, edited by S. Awerbuch, Kluwer Academic Publishers.

Foster, Vivien. 1999. "Non-Price Issues In Utility Regulation: Performance Standards and Social Considerations." Presentation at the International Training Program on Utility Regulation and Strategy, June 2, Public Utilities Research Center, University of Florida.

Gee, Dennis. 2001. "Performance-Based Ratemaking and Business Strategy Implications." Presentation at Infocast, Inc., December conference, Washington, D.C. Available at www.informationforecast.com.

Godbole, Madhave. 2002. "Electricity Regulatory Commissions: The Jury Is Still Out." *Economic and Political Weekly*, Vol. XXXVII, No 7.

Gomez-Ibanez, Jose A. 1999. *The Future of Private Infrastructure: Lessons From the Nationalization of Electric Utilities In Latin America, 1943-1970.* Discussion Paper, Taubman Center, Kennedy School of Government, Harvard University.

Gray, Philip. 2003. "What We Know About Foreign Exchange and Tariff Adjustment in Relation to Macro Shocks." *Viewpoint*, World Bank Finance, Private Sector and Infrastructure Network Forthcoming. See www.worldbank.org/html/fpd/notes.

Green, Richard, 1999. "Checks and Balances in Utility Regulation—The U.K. Experience," *Viewpoint*, Number 185, World Bank Finance, Private Sector and Infrastructure Network. Available at www1.worldbank.org/viewpoint/HTMLNotes/185/185summary.html.

Guasch, J. Luis, Jean-Jacques Laffont and Stephane Straub. 2002. "Renegotiation of Concession Contracts in Latin America." Research Paper No. C02-22, University of Southern California Center for Law, Economics and Organization.

Guasch, J. Luis. 2000. "Lessons from Ten Years of Concessions: Determinants of Performance." Unpublished paper presented at the World Bank, June.

Gupta, Pankaj, Ranjit Lamech, Farida Mazhar and Joseph Wright. 2002. *Mitigating Regulatory Risk for Distribution Privatization: The World Bank Partial Risk Guarantee.* World Bank Energy and Mining Sector Board Discussion Paper Series, No. 5. Available at www.worldbank.org/energy/subenergy/sectorboard_papers.html.

Harris, Clive. 2002. "Private Rural Power: Network Expansion Using Output Based Aid." *Viewpoint*, The World Bank Finance, Private Sector and Infrastructure Network, Note 245.

Houston, Greg and Chris Bowley. 2000. "The Use of Arbitration to Resolve Regulatory Disputes: A Case Study." Unpublished paper. National Economic Research Associates, Sydney, Australia.

Howard, Phillip K. 1996. *The Death of Common Sense: How Law Is Suffocating the United States.* Random House.

Hunt, Sally. 2002. *Making Competition Work in Electricity.* John Wiley and Sons.

Jacobs, Scott. 1994. *Building Regulatory Institutions: The Search for Legitimacy and Efficiency.* OECD, Centre for Cooperation with Economies in Transition, Paris.

Kerf, Michel, et al., 1998. *Concessions for Infrastructure: A Guide to their Design and Award.* World Bank Technical Paper No. 399. Available at http://rru.worldbank.org/Toolkits/concessions.

Lamech, Ranjit and Kazeem Saeed. 2003. *2002 Survey of Power Sector Investors in Developing Countries.* World Bank Energy and Mining Sector Board, Discussion Paper Series. Available at: www.worldbank.org/energy/.

Lawrence, Georgina. 2002. *Who Regulates the Regulator?* Occasional Paper, Centre For The Study of Regulated Industries, University of Bath, England.

Levy, Brian and Pablo Spiller. 1994. "The Institutional Foundations of Regulatory Commitment: A Comparative Analysis of Telecommunications Regulation." *Journal of Law and Economics,* Volume 10(2):201-247.

Lim, Ed. 2001. Speech by World Bank Country Director at conference on Distribution Reforms, October 12, New Delhi, India.

Maurer, Luiz T.A. 2001. "The 'Virtuous Circle' of Contracting." Institute of Americas Conference on Gas and Power Market Convergence, June 25, Rio de Janeiro,.

Mayer, Colin and John Vickers. 1996. "Profit Sharing: An Economic Appraisal." *Fiscal Studies,* Volume 17(2):83-101.

Mercados Energeticos. 2002. *Analysis of Resolution 073/2002 of the Energy Regulatory Comission of Colombia.* In Spanish.

Michaels, Robert. 1996. "Stranded Investments, Stranded Intellectuals." *Regulation,* 1996, Number 1.

Monari, Lucio. 2002. "Power Subsidies: A Reality Check on Subsidizing Power for Irrigation in India." *Viewpoint,* Number 244, The World Bank, Private Sector and Infrastructure Network. Available at www.worldbank.org/viewpoint/HTMLNotes/244/244summary.html.

Nellis, John. 2002. "Effects of Privatization on Income and Wealth Distribution." Paper presented at the World Bank, November. Available at www.rru.worldbank.org.

OFGEM. 1999. *Reviews of Public Electricity Suppliers 1998 to 2000, Supply Price Controls, Final Proposals.* Available at www.ofgem.gov.uk/.

Plummer, James and Susan Troppman, eds. 1990. *Competition In Electricity New Markets and New Structures.* Public Utilities Reports, Inc.

Procta, Mark. 2001. Presentation by Program and Project Supervisor, Office of Ratepayer Advocates, California Public Utilities Commission at a conference on "Performance-Based Ratemaking and Business Strategy Implications," Infocast, Inc., December, Washington, D.C. Available at www.informationforecast.com.

Putman, Robert D. 1993. *Making Democracy Work: Civic Traditions In Modern Italy.* Princeton, New Jersey: Princeton University Press.

Raab, Jonathan, 1994. *Using Consensus Building to Improve Utility Regulation.* Washington, D.C., and Berkeley, California: American Council for an Energy-Efficient Economy.

Rao, S. L. 2001. "The Last Resort." *PowerLine,* December.

Rudnick, Hugh and Jorge A. Donoso. 2000. "Integration of Price Cap and Yardstick Competition Schemes in Electrical Distribution Regulation." *IEEE Transactions on Power Systems,* Volume 15(4):1428-1433.

Sagar, Jagdish. 2002. "DVB Restructuring and Privatisation of Distribution in Delhi." Unpublished paper given at the World Bank, August.

Samarajiva, Rohan. 2001. "Establishing Regulatory Legitimacy." In *Proceedings of the SAFIR Workshop on Regulatory Strategy,* edited by S. K. Sarkar, New Delhi: Tata Energy Research Institute on behalf of SAFIR (South Asian Forum For Infrastructure Regulation). Available at www.safir.teri.res.in/wkshp/legalproceed.pdf.

Schwartz, Eric and Jan Paulson. 1999. "Confronting Political and Regulatory Risks Associated with Private Investment in Developing Countries: The Role of International Dispute Settlement Mechanisms." Paper presented at the Conference on Private Infrastructure for Development: Confronting Political and Regulatory Risk, September 8-10, Rome, Italy. Available at www.worldbank.org/html/fpd/risk/papers.htm.

Shugart, Chris. 1998. "Regulation-by-Contract and Municipal Services: The Problem of Contractual Incompleteness." Ph.D. thesis, Harvard University.

Shuttleworth, Graham. 1999. " 'Regulatory Benchmarking': A Way Forward or a Dead End?" *Energy Regulation Brief,* National Economic Research Associates. Available at www.nera.com.

Smith, Warrick. 1997. "Utility Regulators: The Independence Debate," *Viewpoint* No. 127, World Bank Finance, Private Sector and Infrastructure Network. Available at www.worldbank.org/html/fpd/notes/ .

Stern, Jon and J. R. Davis. 1999. "Economic Reforms of the Electricity Industries of Central and Eastern Europe." *Economics of Transition,* Volume 6(2):427-460.

Tendler, Judith. 1968. *Electric Power in Brazil: Entrepeneurship in the Public Sector.* Cambridge, Massachusetts: Harvard University Press.

Transparency International. 2002. *Corruption in South Asia—Insights and Benchmarks from Citizen Feedback Surveys in Five Countries.*

Viscusi, W. Kip, John M. Vernon and Joseph E. Harrington, Jr. 2000. *Economics of Regulation and Antitrust.* Third Edition. The MIT Press.

Williamson, Oliver E. 1983. "Credible Commitments: Using Hostages to Support Exchange." *American Economic Review,* Volume 73.

Woolf, Fiona and Jon Halpern. 2001. "Integrating Independent Power Producers into Emerging Wholesale Power Markets." The World Bank, Policy Research Working Paper No. 2703. Available at www.econ.worldbank.org.

World Bank, Project Finance and Guarantee Department. *IDA Guarantee Catalyses Private Finance for Haripur Power Project in Bangladesh.* April 2002. Available at www.worldbank.org/guarantees/publications.

___. 1995. *Bureaucrats In Business: The Economics and Politics of Government Ownership.* World Bank Policy Research Report, Oxford University Press.

___. 1993. *The World Bank's Role in the Electric Power Sector.* World Bank Policy Paper, Washington, D.C.

Wright, Joseph. 2003. "Mitigating Foreign Exchange Risk in Private Power Investments in Developing Countries." Forthcoming in the World Bank Energy and Mining Discussion Paper series. Will be available at www.worldbank.org/energy.